OXFORD
INDIA SHORT
INTRODUCTIONS

JAWAHARLAL NEHRU

The Oxford India Short
Introductions are concise,
stimulating, and accessible guides
to different aspects of India.
Combining authoritative analyses,
new ideas, and diverse perspectives,
they discuss subjects which are
topical yet enduring, as also
emerging areas of study and debate.

T0364631

For more information visit our website:
https://india.oup.com/content/series/o/
oxford-india-short-introductions/

OXFORD
INDIA SHORT
INTRODUCTIONS

JAWAHARLAL NEHRU

RUDRANGSHU
MUKHERJEE

OXFORD
UNIVERSITY PRESS

OXFORD
UNIVERSITY PRESS

Oxford University Press is a department of the University of Oxford.
It furthers the University's objective of excellence in research, scholarship,
and education by publishing worldwide. Oxford is a registered trademark of
Oxford University Press in the UK and in certain other countries.

Published in India by
Oxford University Press
2/11 Ground Floor, Ansari Road, Daryaganj, New Delhi 110 002, India

ISBN-13 (print edition): 978-0-19-949295-4
ISBN-10 (print edition): 0-19-949295-6

ISBN-13 (eBook): 978-0-19-909659-6
ISBN-10 (eBook): 0-19-909659-7

Typeset in 11/14.3 Bembo Std
by Digiultrabooks Pvt. Ltd., New Delhi 110 096
Printed in India by Replika Press Pvt. Ltd

In gratitude to
Ashish Dhawan
Pramath Raj Sinha
Sanjeev Bickchandani
Vineet Gupta

who lit up a few moments in my life by
bringing me to Ashoka University

Contents

Abbreviations

A	Jawaharlal Nehru, *An Autobiography*
DoI	Jawaharlal Nehru, *The Discovery of India*
JNSW	Jawaharlal Nehru, *Selected Works*
JNEW	Jawaharlal Nehru, *Essential Writings*
GWH	Jawaharlal Nehru, *Glimpses of World History*
CWMG	*Collected Works of Mahatma Gandhi*
FIJN	S. Gopal, 'The Formative Ideology of Jawaharlal Nehru'.

Introduction

Jawaharlal Nehru, India's first prime minister, was born in 1889 in the north Indian town of Allahabad. His father, Motilal, was a highly successful lawyer. The Nehrus were Kashmiri Pundits who had migrated to the United Provinces of Agra and Oudh (present-day Uttar Pradesh)—first to Agra, and then to Allahabad, where they settled down. Jawaharlal was born into luxury. His father's house had a private swimming pool and a tennis court; there was a large retinue of servants who doted on Jawaharlal, the eldest born and male heir. Motilal had adopted a westernized style of living and wanted to bring up his only son in the model of an upper-class English gentleman.

As a young boy, Jawaharlal was educated at home by an English tutor, from whom he imbibed an interest in science and a lifelong passion for reading. In 1905, Motilal admitted his son to Harrow. Away from home, Jawaharlal adapted himself to the ways of an English public school, studying and participating in games and other activities of the school. He was not particularly happy at Harrow, but did reasonably well in his studies, occasionally winning prizes. His headmaster wrote in one of his reports, 'Nehru is not without brains'. Jawaharlal then decided to move to Trinity College, Cambridge, because he felt he had mentally outgrown Harrow. At Trinity, he opted for the Natural Sciences Tripos. He got a reasonably good degree. He rowed for the college, rode, and became a member of the college debating society, Magpie and Stump. He was a shy young man and not a very successful debater. Even though his academic career at Harrow and Cambridge was not marked by any remarkable success, both institutions left deep impressions on him.

While he was up at Trinity, Jawaharlal was also called to the bar from Lincoln's Inn. He returned to India in 1912 with the expectation that he would wear the barrister-at-law's silk gown and take on his father's lucrative practice. Back in India, he married a girl chosen by his parents. His bride Kamala (nee Kaul) came from a distinguished family of Kashmiri pundits, but her background was very different from that of the westernized Nehrus. She came from a more traditional family, spoke no English, and was completely unfamiliar with English social etiquette and table manners. After the marriage was arranged, Motilal brought Kamala to

Allahabad and placed her under an English governess to have her trained in the Western modes of living so that she could be a proper partner for Jawaharlal. This gap between Jawaharlal and Kamala was never to be breached.

However, he never became the successful lawyer his father expected him to be. For a few years after his return, he drifted through the social life of Allahabad, and out of curiosity, attended sessions of the Indian National Congress. Jawaharlal found them to be useless and described them as a rich man's tea parties. He even met Mohandas Karamchand Gandhi once, and found him to be cold and distant.

The massacre at Jallianwala Bagh was to change everything for Jawaharlal. He was appointed a member of the Enquiry Committee of the Indian National Congress to investigate what had actually happened at Jallianwala Bagh. The head of the committee was Chittaranjan Das, a leading figure of the Congress. Jawaharlal made detailed notes of what he had seen and heard in Amritsar (JNSW: 1: 130–40). The Committee's findings opened Jawaharlal's eyes to the nature of the British rule and the violence it embodied. He wrote about this in October 1919 in *The Bombay Chronicle*. Jawaharlal was convinced that India had no future unless it could rid itself of a regime that he considered barbaric. There was no turning back for Jawaharlal from this point. He joined the national movement, which was in the process of being radically transformed under the leadership of Gandhi. From 1920 to 1947, Jawaharlal's life was completely devoted to the Indian National Movement and the Congress. He began as a worker and rose to be a leader whose standing and popularity was second only to Gandhi's.

Chapter 1 of this book looks at this formative experience of Jawaharlal and how it provided him with a perspective on Indian history and the people of India. It was an experience that he recollected vividly in *An Autobiography*; his recollections of what he described as 'wandering among the kisans' left its mark on his book, *The Discovery of India*. An important aspect of Jawaharlal's transformation from a westernized young man to a convinced nationalist and Congressman was his almost accidental exposure to the world of the peasants of north India. He came to be involved in a large-scale peasant movement in southeastern Awadh, a few miles into the countryside from his hometown of Allahabad. He spoke to the peasants, learnt about their life and grievances, and witnessed their poverty. He occasionally stayed with them as he travelled extensively across the area. It was his first discovery of India and an experience that he never forgot.

Chapter 2 looks at Nehru as a leader of the Congress and his political views. From 1929, when he was elected as the president of the Congress for the first time, Jawaharlal became an integral part of the leadership of the Congress, which was leading the Indian National Movement. Within the party, he developed his own ideology and political views that were often out of tune with what the other leaders were advocating. Thus, in spite of being close to Gandhi and with other Congress leaders, his relationship with the Congress was never easy. During the 1930s, Jawaharlal visited Europe a number of times for personal reasons, and the rise of fascism and socialism informed his emerging ideology. He also became increasingly conscious that India's struggle for freedom was part of a wider historical process in which many Asian and African countries were trying to liberate themselves from colonial rule. This kind of awareness gave his ideology a distinctive dimension that was often not shared by other Congress leaders, including Gandhi. This chapter also reviews the role that Jawaharlal played in the crucial negotiations that resulted in the partition of India.

Chapter 3 is an analysis of Jawaharlal's unique relationship with Gandhi. No one was more articulate than Jawaharlal in his criticism of Gandhi's fundamental views about India, its past and its future. Yet no one was as close to Gandhi as he was. This chapter attempts to recollect this tension-fraught but profoundly affectionate relationship between the two men.

Chapter 4 surveys the career of Jawaharlal as the first prime minister of India. It does so by looking under distinct heads at his work between 1947 and 1964 when he died: first, the steps he took as the architect of India's democratic structure to ensure democratic norms and practices; second, his attempts to make India a self-sufficient economy through a process of socialist planning; and third, the direction he gave to Indian foreign policy.

The concluding chapter of the book attempts to make an overall assessment of Jawaharlal as a political leader—as a prime minister and as a man. It also highlights some of the lasting legacies of what has come to be known as 'the Nehru era'.

1

Discovery of Indians

Commenting on his own political consciousness and attitudes during his growing up years, Jawaharlal wrote with candour in his autobiography: 'My politics had been those of my class, the bourgeoisie ... I was totally ignorant of labour conditions in factories and fields' (A: 48–9). He had no direct knowledge of or exposure to the poverty of the common people of India. This changed in the most unexpected way. In June 1920, 300–500 peasants led by a preacher, who called himself Baba Ram Chandra came to Allahabad from the interior villages of Pratapgarh and Jaunpur. They wanted to meet some prominent politicians, perhaps even Gandhi, and draw their attention to the miserable plight of the peasants in southeastern Awadh. Jawaharlal learnt that the peasants were squatting on one of the *ghats* of the Jamuna, and went to meet them. It was from this meeting that Jawaharlal first learnt what conditions some of the peasants of Awadh lived in, and the power the *taluqdars* (very large landlords) wielded over them. The peasants wanted Jawaharlal to come with them and see for himself. Jawaharlal travelled to the interiors of Awadh two days later.

This was the first of many visits that transformed his consciousness. The villages he visited were far away from a railway station, and some of them distant even from a *pucca* road. What Jawaharlal saw was a revelation to him: his first exposure to the rural reality of India. What he witnessed was a 'whole countryside afire with enthusiasm and full of a strange excitement' (A: 52). Unknown to him, Jawaharlal had landed in the midst of a large-scale peasant movement. In his autobiography, he recalled it in vivid terms:

[E]normous gatherings would take place at the briefest notice by word of mouth. One village would communicate with another and the second with the third, and so on and presently whole villages would empty out, and all over the fields there would be men and women and children on the march to the meeting place. Or, more swiftly still, the cry SitaRam—Sita Ra-a-a-a-m—would fill the air, and travel far in all directions and be echoed back from other villages, and then people would come streaming out or even running as fast as they could. They were in miserable rags, men and women, but their faces were full of excitement and their eyes glistened and seemed to expect strange happenings which would, as if by a miracle, put an end to their long misery.

This exposure to the conditions of the peasantry in southeastern Awadh had a profound impact on Jawaharlal. It was, first and foremost, a revelation. 'It lifted the veil', he would write later in his autobiography, 'and disclosed a fundamental aspect of the Indian problem to which nationalists had paid hardly any attention'. He got to know the wretched condition of the peasants and this left an ineradicable mark on Jawaharlal's mind. To quote again from his autobiography, 'ever since then [his first visits to the villages of Pratapgarh] my mental picture of India always contains this naked, hungry mass'. His idea of India could not be divorced from these people, 'naked, starving, crushed, and utterly miserable' (A: 63, 57, and 52).

Jawaharlal's involvement in the peasant movement also brought him face-to-face with the atrocities of the British administration. In January 1921, just outside Rae Bareli on the banks of the Sai river, he witnessed a firing on a gathering of unnamed peasants. He spent the next few days travelling around the area visiting the wounded and seeing the conditions for himself. This experience, 'wandering among the kisans', as he was to later call it, converted Jawaharlal to the doctrine of non-violence. Immediately after witnessing the firing, he wrote:

> I have had the privilege of working for them, of mixing with them, of living in their mud huts and partaking in all reverence of their lowly fare. And I, who for long believed in the doctrine of the sword, have been converted by the kisans to the doctrine of non-violence. I have come to believe that non-violence is ingrained in them and is part of their very nature ... It is not the masses but we, nurtured in an atmosphere of the West, who talk glibly of the inefficiency of peaceful methods. The masses know the power of *Ahimsa*. (JNSW: 1: 211)

Jawaharlal's baptism in ahimsa happened among the peasants long before Gandhi became an overwhelming influence on his life. This unqualified and immediate admission of his conversion to non-violence in the company of peasants came to be erased in the later reflections and recollections of Jawaharlal. In his later writings, he ascribed his conversion to ahimsa to the spell of Gandhi.

By 1921, Jawaharlal had decided immerse himself in the Non-Cooperation Movement launched by Gandhi. He urged all Indians to do the same. India's freedom became Jawaharlal's calling. He was happy that he was 'crusading for a cause' and 'wholly absorbed in the movement' (A: 69–73). By his own admission, '[I] gave up all my other associations and contacts, old friends, books, even newspapers … In spite of the strength of my family bonds, I almost forgot my family, my wife, my daughter'. Jawaharlal's enthusiastic participation and leadership spurred on the Non-Cooperation Movement in United Provinces, where it had had a disappointing start. Joining the Non-Cooperation Movement brought a new experience to his life.

On 5 December 1921, Jawaharlal was imprisoned by the British government for the first time. Jail would become a recurrent part of his life under the Raj. In the course of the trial that led to his second spell in jail, Jawaharlal made an impassioned statement to the court; the following summed up his attitude to being a guest of His Majesty:

Jail has indeed become a heaven for us, a holy place of pilgrimage since our saintly and beloved leader was sentenced … I marvel at my good fortune. To serve India in the battle of freedom is honour enough … But to suffer for the dear country! What greater good fortune could befall an Indian unless it be death for the cause or the full realization of our glorious dream. (JNSW: 1: 66)

Gandhi's withdrawal of the Non-Cooperation Movement left Jawaharlal dejected and confused. He also found the state of the Congress, as divided as it was into factions and cliques, to be very discouraging. Caught briefly in a political vacuum, a new avenue of work opened up for Jawaharlal. He took to municipal work as the head of the Allahabad municipality. He emphasized work and discipline, and worked tirelessly to improve conditions in schools, public health, and sanitation. Successful though he was in municipal work, it did not really appeal to Jawaharlal's imagination. But family matters drew him away from politics. His wife Kamala was unwell and he himself was recovering from a bad attack of typhoid. In March 1926, he set sail for Europe with Kamala and their daughter, Indira.

In 1926, Europe was on the brink of a transition, and this made the trip to Europe was important for Jawaharlal. It exposed him to new ideas and to historical events as they unfolded in the continent. They helped him to formulate his own ideas about India and her freedom struggle. He taught himself, in the course of this trip, to place India's liberation movement on a wider historical canvas. This was the first time that Jawaharlal met European political workers and witnessed political movements. This experience was enriched by reading certain books, especially Bertrand Russell's *On Education* and *What I Believe*. A critical point in his political and intellectual development was his participation in the International Congress against Colonial Oppression and Imperialism held at Brussels in February 1927. This conference was, as Jawaharlal realized, either sponsored by the Soviet Union or was not-so-covertly supported by it. The conference had one principal purpose: to bring together anti-colonial movements and the organized working class against imperialism, especially British imperialism. The delegates to the conference came from varied backgrounds—European communists, trade unionists, pacifists, and nationalists from Asia, Africa, and Latin America. And of course, given the times, the conference was also attended by secret service agents; sometimes, some delegates doubled up as spies. This conference radicalized Jawaharlal by making him receptive to socialist and Marxist ideas. Jawaharlal's new intellectual orientations were evident in the speech he made at the inaugural session and in the resolution on India, which he drafted. Jawaharlal drew out the close links between imperialism and capitalism. He tried to convey how the two systems functioned in an interlocked manner. Back in India, he brought into the Indian National Movement a dimension that had never been articulated before. He urged the Indian National Congress to push its agenda beyond political freedom: he wanted the Movement's programme to aim for the full emancipation of the peasants and workers of India, 'without which there can be no real freedom'. He added that the liberation movement in India would cooperate with the movements for emancipation across the world. These would be recurring themes in Jawaharlal's speeches and writings in the 1930s and became embedded as crucial elements of his formative ideology.

The Brussels conference also founded the League against Imperialism and For National Independence for greater co-ordination between the various national movements in the colonial countries, and between labour and anti-imperialist movements in the metropolitan countries. Jawaharlal was appointed an honorary president of the League. More than the deliberations of the League and the conference, what really preoccupied Jawaharlal's mind was the Soviet Union. He read everything he could about the Soviet Union—its ideology, policies, and conditions. He found a lot to admire in the Soviet Union, although he foresaw the possibility of it developing its own form of imperialism as it grew in power and influence. For the moment, he believed that the Soviet Union—out of self-interest—was supporting the anti-colonial movements (JNSW: 2: 348–64). He was very keen to visit the country, and in November 1927, he did. He was greatly impressed by what he saw especially

14

by the progress the Soviet Union had made in areas like agriculture, prison reform, the elimination of inequality, the condition of women, and the eradication of illiteracy. He wrote to his sister from there that he was 'in topsy turvy land. All one's old values get upset and life wears a strange aspect here' (JNSW: 2: 369).

Today, with the wisdom of hindsight, it is easy to criticize Jawaharlal's glib admiration for the Soviet Union. He was on a conducted tour and saw only what he was allowed to see. Jawaharlal's reaction to the Soviet Union was by no means unique in the late 1920s and 1930s. For many who were disillusioned with capitalism and imperialism found in the Soviet Union the potentialities of a new civilization that was less unequal and more liberating than what capitalism had come to represent in the first decades of the twentieth century. This was the illusion of the epoch—the Soviet Union as the harbinger of hope. Jawaharlal fell prey to this illusion.

When Jawaharlal returned to India at the end of 1927, his political and ideological orientation was different from what he had imbued from Gandhi. He would always be devoted Gandhi but he would never again completely accept Gandhi's ideology without question and criticism. Europe had taught him to look at India and the world in radically different terms. He best summed up his altered understanding: 'My outlook was wider, and nationalism by itself seemed to me definitely a narrow and insufficient creed. Political freedom, independence, were no doubt essential, but they were steps in the right direction; without social freedom and socialistic structure and the State, neither the country nor the individual could develop much' (A: 166).

The difference in attitude was immediately noticeable in Jawaharlal's political activities in India. He had come to believe that the Congress should have only one aim—complete independence from British rule— and had a resolution passed in the Madras session of the Congress at the end of 1927 announcing 'the goal of the Indian people to be complete independence'. He wrote to Gandhi that the idea of Dominion Status, to which the Congress was then committed, suffocated and strangled him (JNSW: 3: 12). Gandhi considered the resolution demanding independence to be a 'tragedy' (CWMG: 3: 3–4). The Congress leadership did not take the resolution seriously, and Jawaharlal was disappointed. Together with Subhas Bose, he formed the Independence for India League and used this forum to spread the idea of complete independence and his idea of a socialist India.

Jawaharlal's commitment to serve the cause of India's independence was tested on the ground when he was involved in the movement to boycott the Simon Commission that had come to India in early 1928. During a peaceful demonstration against the Commission in November 1928 in Lucknow, Jawaharlal was beaten up by the police on two separate occasions. This was the first time Jawaharlal had been beaten up by the police, and the bodily pain not only made him morally tougher but strengthened his resolution as well. He recalled the experience vividly in his autobiography: 'The bodily pain I felt was quite forgotten in a feeling of exhilaration that I was physically strong enough to face and bear lathi blows. And a thing that surprised me was that right through the incident, even when I was being beaten, my mind was quite clear and I was consciously analyzing my feelings' (A: 178–80). The violence inflicted upon him by the police convinced him that the only sanction that British rule had in India was physical force. He told the press that the violence of the police on a peaceful crowd only highlighted 'the real issue before the people of the country ... that issue is that British rule in India means the policeman's baton and the bayonet and the real problem is how to overcome them' (JNSW: 3: 108–15). He had imbibed from Gandhi, his chosen leader, the lesson that the only way this sanction could be subverted was through non-violence.

Given his emerging socialist ideology, it was not surprising that he involved himself in youth and working-class movements. At the end of 1928 he travelled to Poona, where he addressed the Bombay Presidency Youth Conference. He spoke to the students about the links between imperialism and capitalism, and about the need for the reconstruction of society on another basis, socialism. He also went to Jharia to attend the annual session of the All India Trade Union Congress. He felt like an outsider there, as it was the first time that he attended a trade union congress. Here too, Jawaharlal came face-to-face with the oppressive nature of the British rule. During the congress, the police walked in to arrest W.J. Johnston, who was attending as a delegate from the League against Imperialism. Jawaharlal forced the police to leave the premises. Johnston was arrested the next day outside the venue, leading to a denunciation by Jawaharlal of the British rule and imperialism.

Jawaharlal's growing radicalism led him to espouse the cause of those who had been arrested in the Meerut Conspiracy case. One of his tasks was to arrange for the best legal defence for the prisoners. His efforts in this regard did not prove successful as he discovered that the best lawyers were not interested in a case that would not be very lucrative.

These activities faded into relative insignificance in the context of the role Jawaharlal assumed within the Congress. He was appointed president of the

Congress for 1929 session in Lahore, but this elevation was not without a touch of controversy. Motilal had been trying to persuade Gandhi since 1927 to make Jawaharlal the president. Gandhi had resisted until 1929 when three names were considered: Gandhi himself, Vallabhbhai Patel, and Jawaharlal. In the voting, Gandhi secured ten, Patel five, and Jawaharlal three. Gandhi was declared elected but he resigned and wanted a younger person to lead to inspire the youth of India (Sitaramayya: 1: 347). A very unwilling Jawaharlal was pitch-forked into the presidency. He wrote to Gandhi: 'My personal inclination always is not to be shackled down to any office ... I represent nobody but myself. I have not the politician's flair for forming groups ... Most people who put me forward for the presidentship do so because they want to keep someone else out ... This kind of negative backing is hardly good enough ...' (JNSW: 4: 156–7). But Gandhi prevailed, and perhaps made matters worse by writing in *Young India* that making Jawaharlal president was as good as making Gandhi the president. He thus implied that Jawaharlal was his creature or his mirror image. Looking back on this episode, Jawaharlal wrote in his autobiography:

> I have seldom felt quite so annoyed and humiliated as I did at that election. It was not that I was not sensible of the honour, for it was a great honour ...

But I did not come to it by the main entrance or even a side entrance; I appeared suddenly by a trap-door and bewildered the audience into acceptance ... My pride was hurt, and almost I felt like handing back the honour. Fortunately I restrained myself from making an exhibition of myself, and stole away with a heavy heart. (A: 194–5)

There was another and a different kind of discomfiture lurking around the corner for the president-elect, Jawaharlal. In October 1929, the viceroy, Lord Irwin, issued what he called a Declaration, which was based on some informal discussion that he had had with some Congress leaders like Motilal Nehru and Tej Bahadur Sapru. The Declaration stated that His Majesty's government had come to the conclusion that 'the natural issue of India's constitutional progress ... is the attainment of Dominion Status' (Roberts [1991] 2004). Given this, the government wanted to invite 'representatives of different parties and interests' to a Round Table Conference in London to discuss new constitutional proposals for India with British political leaders. Jawaharlal was sceptical of the government's intentions and drafted a resolution that noted that 'there is no assurance in it that our demands will be acceded to in the near future'.

Meanwhile at a meeting of some members of the Working Committee, a different draft known as the

Delhi Manifesto was adopted. The Manifesto ran completely contrary to what Jawaharlal had expressed. It promised full co-operation, with certain conditions, to the government in its efforts to find a scheme of Dominion constitution for India. Jawaharlal signed the manifesto with great reluctance after Gandhi told him he could not remain a member of the Working Committee and president of the Congress if he had such major differences with his colleagues. He wrote to Gandhi about his disappointment and, in fact, offered to resign. Gandhi wrote back, consoling him and telling him that if he resigned at that juncture, it would affect the national cause. The controversy blew over as the British government refused to accept the Delhi Manifesto.

Things were smooth when Jawaharlal, as the new president, rode into the Congress session on a white charger amidst tumultuous applause. Jawaharlal's presidential address was unlike any other speech from a Congress president. He began by placing India's independence in an international context. He predicted with some confidence that European domination of the world was nearing its end, and that already, 'Europe had ceased to be the centre of activity and interest'. India was part of a global movement, in which China, Turkey, Persia, Egypt, and even the Soviet Union were participants. It could not remain isolated. India had a message to give to the world, but 'she [had] also to receive and learn much from the messages of other peoples'. The other themes that Jawaharlal expounded were economic equality and liberty, without which, he argued, India's social structure would have no stability. Economic equality would have to be an integral struggle to achieve complete political independence from British rule. He also announced his own creed very boldly: 'I am a socialist and a republican, and am no believer in kings and princes, or in the order which produces the modern kings of industry, who have greater power over the lives and fortunes of men than even the kings of old' (JNSW: 4: 184–98).

As the 1930s decade began, Jawaharlal was poised to enter a new phase in his political career, his own intellectual development, and even his personal life. He was now fully involved in the Congress-led national movement but he had also declared his own ideological position that was not altogether congruent with the views held by the Congress leadership, including Gandhi. He had been among the *kisans*, had been in prison, and had suffered physical pain at the hands of the police. He had fallen under the spell of Gandhi, a spell that he often did not understand. But he was conscious that Gandhi was bringing to the national movement a dimension that was unique. Thus, when Gandhi inaugurated the Civil Disobedience Movement in March 1930, Jawaharlal, as he later confessed, was at first 'bewildered' and 'could not quite fit in a national struggle with common salt'. But salt in the hands of Gandhi 'suddenly became a mysterious word, a word of power' (A: 218). Jawaharlal was perceptive enough to recognize that Gandhi had brought to his life and to the lives of thousands of other Indians 'something of epic greatness' (Iyengar and Zackariah 2011: 122–4). He could never erase from his mind the image of Gandhi during the Dandi March. Many years later, he recalled that picture:

Many pictures rise in my mind of this man, whose eyes were often full of laughter and yet were pools of infinite sadness. But the picture that is dominant and most significant is as I saw him marching staff in hand, to Dandi on the Salt March in 1930. He was the pilgrim on his quest of truth, quiet, peaceful, determined and fearless, who could continue that quiet pilgrimage regardless of consequences. ('Foreword', Tendulkar [1951])

2

Leader of the Congress

This new phase of Jawaharlal's life began on a note of optimism, but was very soon overtaken by disappointment and death. Jawaharlal observed Gandhi's march to the sea and proceeded to prepare the party workers for the Civil Disobedience Movement. He campaigned in rural United Provinces, and a few days before Gandhi broke the salt monopoly, Jawaharlal wrote to a British correspondent: 'There is no doubt that India is awake and astir and we are going to give a good fight to the British government ... Somehow I cannot help thinking that the days of the British empire are numbered now' (JNSW: 4: 298–9). As the movement started, Jawaharlal was out in Allahabad and other parts of the United Provinces selling salt, while at the same time in Rae Bareli, he was organizing peasants for the non-payment of rent. The British government was quick to respond to these activities—in the middle of April 1930, Jawaharlal was arrested and imprisoned in Naini Central Jail for six months. The charge was that he had helped in the manufacture of salt.

The routine of jail life—exercise, reading, and writing—was broken only by Jawaharlal's refusal to accept special privileges (food from home, a *punkha*, and so on) and by the arrival of his father, who was also sentenced to serve a prison term. Confined in prison, Jawaharlal was completely cut off from what was happening in the theatre of the national movement, where not only had the call for civil disobedience galvanized the people, but there were stirring movements outside the Gandhian non-violent struggle. On 23 April 1930 in Chittagong, a group of armed revolutionaries under Surya Sen captured the local armoury, issued an Independence Proclamation, and fought a pitched battle against the British forces. In spite of the very different mode of challenging the British government that the revolutionaries adopted, they declared their triumph with the cry 'Gandhi raj has come'. On the same day as the Chittagong uprising, Peshawar fell out of British control through a popular insurgency, where Hindu soldiers refused to fire on Muslim crowds. It took the British ten days to regain control over Peshawar. On 7 May, Gandhi was arrested, triggering a textile strike in Sholapur, Bombay

Province, and in response to it, crowds attacked liquor shops, police outposts, and government buildings. Jawaharlal heard about the Peshawar and the Sholapur uprisings in prison.

The growing discontent among the people triggered increased government repression—a consequence was that martial law had to be imposed. The uprising might also have initiated negotiations to find a settlement. Before his arrest, Motilal Nehru might have been instrumental in beginning a truce process, but he expressed regret in prison to his son for having conveyed the impression that the Congress was open to a compromise. The real authors of the compromise were Tej Bahadur Sapru and M.R. Jayakar, who were known as the liberals within the Congress. Sapru and Jayakar met Gandhi in Yerwada Jail in late July. Gandhi gave them a note for the Nehrus in Naini prison, along with a separate letter for Motilal. In the note, Gandhi said that the Round Table Conference should be restricted to a discussion of the safeguards necessary in connection with self-government during the transition period (Sitarammaya: 1: 637–8). In the letter to Motilal, Gandhi expressed his grave doubts as to whether the time was right for an honourable settlement. But he wanted the final decision to be Jawaharlal's. 'You and I can only give our advice to him', he told Motilal. He added that the note he had sent through Sapru and Jayakar expressed 'the utmost to which I can go', and that he was open to a 'stronger position' (Mukherjee 2014: 91). The response of the Nehrus, father and son, to the overtures of Sapru and Jayakar was far from positive. In a joint memorandum, Jawaharlal and Motilal made it clear that they could not take any decision from within prison where they could not consult any of their colleagues, especially Gandhi. Jawaharlal wrote separately to Gandhi. In that letter, he made it clear that neither he nor his father accepted Gandhi's position on the constitutional issue, but that they agreed with Gandhi that there could be no truce that would undo the present position that the national movement represented under the Congress. Jawaharlal was pessimistic about any settlement and was unwilling to issue any statement as the Congress president, since that move could be misinterpreted as a weakness. He clearly expressed his own state of mind: 'I delight in warfare. It makes me feel that I am alive. Events of the last four months in India have gladdened my heart and have made me prouder of Indian men, women and even children than I had ever been ...' (JNSW: 4: 369–70).

As a result of all this activity, Motilal, Jawaharlal, and Syed Mahmud were taken by a special train to Yerwada, where a meeting was held in which Sapru, Jayakar, Gandhi, Vallabhbhai Patel, Sarojini Naidu, and

Jairamdas Doulatram were also present. The Congress leaders signed a memorandum on 15 August that stated that the time was not ripe for a settlement that would be honourable for India. They emphasized the fact that they could observe 'no symptom of conversion of the English official world to the view that it is India's men and women who must decide what is best for India'. Nevertheless, the Congress leaders said a settlement was possible if the British government (*a*) recognized India's right to secede from the British Empire, and (*b*) gave to India a complete national government responsible to her people, including control over defence and the economy (Sitarammaya: 1: 641–2). Lord Irwin, the viceroy, found these conditions unacceptable, and on 31 August, the Nehrus wrote from Naini prison to Gandhi to inform him that the efforts of Sapru and Jayakar were all for naught.

The course of these discussion and negotiations revealed an important aspect that did not escape the notice of top British officials. The secretary of state for India, Wedgewood Benn, wrote to the viceroy that he had been struck by 'Gandhi's deference to Jawaharlal and Jawaharlal's pride in what had been achieved as well as his declaration of belief in non-violence. It was the apparent pride which depressed me, because it did not show the spirit of a beaten man' (Gopal: 1: 146). British administrators were forced to accept that another voice and view were emerging in India, different from Gandhi's.

The emergence of Jawaharlal as an important figure in the Congress leadership had no impact on the immediate turn of events. In March 1931, much to the surprise and bewilderment of Jawaharlal, the Civil Disobedience movement was withdrawn by the announcement of the Gandhi–Irwin Pact. Jawaharlal, who was in Delhi at that time after being released from prison, had observed the steps leading up to the pact. The pact had a very adverse effect on Jawaharlal, leaving him in 'great mental and physical distress' (A: 257–60). He expressed his sense of disappointment and disillusionment to Gandhi in no uncertain terms. In his autobiography, he recorded his feelings regarding the pact:

> The thing had been done, our leader had committed himself; and even if we disagreed with him, what could we do? Throw him over? Break from him? Announce our disagreement? That might bring some personal satisfaction to an individual, but it made no final difference to the final decision ... in my heart there was a great emptiness as of something precious gone, almost beyond recall.
> 'This is the way the world ends,
> Not with a bang but a whimper'.

Even before this demoralization had set in, Jawaharlal had to cope with his father's death. In prison, especially after the negotiations with Sapru and Jayakar, Jawaharlal had watched with alarm the precipitous decline in his father's health. Motilal was released from prison on 8 September, but never recovered. Jawaharlal was released in early October, but this reprieve lasted for only eight days. This spell in prison was a terrible time for him as he knew his father was dying and he could not be with him. Motilal passed away on 6 February 1931, leaving Jawaharlal bereft. Reluctant as always to show his personal emotions in public, Jawaharlal did not express his sense of loss. He had had serious political differences with his father, but had always been conscious of his profound dependence on him. Over time, Jawaharlal had come to value his father's 'sheltering wisdom' (Gopal: 1: 150). He believed that if Motilal had been alive, he could have intervened in the making of the Gandhi–Irwin Pact, which was signed one month after his death. A month after the pact, back in prison, Jawaharlal noted in his diary: 'Always when thinking of the truce people start guessing what might have happened if father had been there and there appears to be a general consensus that events would have taken a very different turn. Foolishly I said so in Delhi a few hours after the truce. How Bapu was pained at my remark!' (JNSW: 5: 363).

While Jawaharlal was in and out of prison, his wife's health had been deteriorating rapidly. Kamala Nehru had never been in the pink of health ever since she had been diagnosed with tuberculosis in 1919. It was never cured despite long spells of treatment. In 1925, she also had to bear the death of a son, born prematurely and alive for only two days; in 1928, she had suffered a miscarriage. Her frail health notwithstanding, she had joined the national movement. In the middle of 1934, she needed urgent medical attention, and Jawaharlal was let out of prison on parole and sent back to jail after eleven days after Kamala showed some improvement. In October that year, she had to be moved to a sanatorium in Bhowali. Under a special dispensation, Jawaharlal was moved to a jail in Almora near Bhowali. The treatment in the sanatorium did not improve matters, and it was evident that she would have to be moved to Europe for medical treatment. Jawaharlal had to dip into his savings to finance this trip. He was in financial difficulties, but turned down the offer from a member of the Birla family to pay him a monthly subsistence. Kamala underwent an operation in Berlin, but her condition did not improve; indeed, it continued to deteriorate. Jawaharlal was released from jail and allowed to travel to Europe. He rushed to Badenweiler in the Black Forest region, where Kamala was being treated at a clinic. From there she was moved

31

to Lausanne in January 1936, where she died in the early morning of 28 February. Jawaharlal was desolated by his wife's death. The British communist leader, R.P. Dutt, who met Jawaharlal around this time, said in an interview that 'with her death some of his backbone went out of him' (Gopal: 1: 195). Jawaharlal always kept a photograph of Kamala and a small portion of her ashes in his bedroom and in his jail cell; he left the request that the ashes be mingled with his own after his death. Theirs had not been an easy marriage, but her death devastated Jawaharlal. His sense of unredeemable loss was articulated a few months later in the austere but poignant dedication to *An Autobiography*: 'To Kamala who is no more'.

Around the time of Kamala's death, Jawaharlal received the news that he had been elected president of the Congress by a massive majority. The proposal to make him the president had come from Gandhi. On the day Jawaharlal was leaving for Europe, Gandhi wrote to him: 'Unless there is an insuperable bar you should take charge of the Congress ship next year'. A more direct request followed a few days later: 'I would like you to allow yourself to be elected President for the next year. Your acceptance will solve many difficulties'. He requested Jawaharlal to permit him to put his name forward for 'the crown of thorns' (Iyengar and Zackariah 2011: 232, 238, and 245). Jawaharlal was initially reluctant as he did not want to be burdened with the responsibilities of office. He warned Gandhi that he was 'apt to behave like a bull in a China shop' (Iyengar and Zackariah 2011: 242–4), but he accepted because, as he explained to Gandhi,

> I do not believe in shirking a job because of difficulties or possibilities of failure. In any event on my return to India I propose to take an active part in politics. They are not for me a career or an occupation from which I can retire at will. Even if I had not had an irrepressible urge towards something, which might not be easy to define, loyalty to the past and even more so to the present, with all its tragic suffering and vulgar suppression of the best in our people, would drive me on. I have little respect for quitters and I hope I shall never be of their number.

His elevation to the presidency of the Congress did not pass without protest. Rajagopalachari expressed his doubts about 'having dreamers and sentimental men in charge of the wheel'. He hoped Jawaharlal would be 'reasonable' and that Gandhi would take the reins (Som 1995: 174–5). The expectation that Jawaharlal would not be his own man was soon to be belied. He was clear about the task that lay before him: to revive the Congress from the torpor into which had sunk after the Civil Disobedience Movement. Moreover, the overall political context had been altered by the Government of India Act of 1935. By this Act, the British government allowed for greater Indian participation at the provincial level while retaining total control in key areas like defence, the economy, and so on. The electorate was increased from 6 million to 30 million. There was no mention, however, of Dominion Status, let alone independence. The Act was seen by the British authorities—in the words of Lord Linlithgow, the viceroy in 1936—as 'the best way ... of maintaining British influence in India ... [and] to hold India to the Empire' (Sarkar 1983: 338). Jawaharlal, like many others in the nationalist leadership including Gandhi, was very critical of the Act. What he underestimated was the number of Congressmen who were lured by the prospect of holding office under the provisions of the Act. Jawaharlal, as president, was thus placed in a changed context and as the leader of a different Congress.

These circumstances did not stop Jawaharlal from delivering a presidential address imbued with the socialist and Marxist ideas that he had imbibed in Europe. He began 'the address by hailing the assembled Congressmen as 'Comrades'. He proceeded to elaborate on what had emerged as one of his pet themes: the placing of India's freedom struggle on a wider map—what was happening elsewhere across

34

the world. An important part of this 'wider picture', according to Jawaharlal, was the fundamental clash between capitalism—of which imperialism was an integral part—and socialism, represented by the new economic and political order in the Soviet Union. Jawaharlal believed that a recent facet of capitalism was fascism, which aimed at the 'brutal suppression of what western civilization had apparently stood for; it became, even in some of its homelands, what its imperialist counterpart had been in the subject colonial countries'. Imperialism and fascism were both different articulations of capitalism, which was now in its death throes. The rising tides of socialism in the West and of nationalism in the East were the twin forces speeding capitalism to its end. But, Jawaharlal warned, fascism was also an expression of nationalism, although of an extreme kind, and was different from the nationalism that was emerging in Asia: 'Nationalism in the East ... was essentially different from the new and terribly narrow nationalism of fascist countries; the former was the historical urge for freedom, the latter the last refuge of reaction'. Returning to the theme of socialism, Jawaharlal saw in it 'the key to the solutions of the world's problems and of India's problems'. He declared that he was a believer in socialism, and wanted the Congress to be a socialist organization and join 'other forces in the world which are working for a new civilization'. He accepted that the Congress was not yet poised to become a socialist organization since it was seized by disunion and petty conflicts. Congress had turned its back on larger ideals and had lost touch with the masses. 'The Congress', Jawaharlal said, 'must not only be *for* the masses, as it claims to be, but *of* the masses; only then will it really be *for* the masses'. Finally, referring to immediate issues, Jawaharlal spoke against accepting office once elections had been held under the Government of India Act of 1935 (JNSW 7: 170–95).

Jawaharlal could not possibly have imagined the storm that his presidential address would unleash within and without the Congress. The majority of the Working Committee, led by Vallabhbhai Patel, C. Rajagopalachari, and Rajendra Prasad, could not accept Jawaharlal's emphasis on socialism. They felt that this was not in the best interests of the country and the national movement, and that Jawaharlal through his speeches had actually weakened the Congress organization. In protest, those three leaders, along with four others, resigned from the Working Committee at Gandhi's suggestion. They later withdrew their resignations on Gandhi's advice. Jawaharlal thus began his presidency by being at loggerheads with his Working Committee.

The winds of protest howled even louder outside the Congress. In the middle of May 1936, twenty-one leading businessmen of Bombay publicly condemned Jawaharlal's championing of socialism. They thought it was subversive and destructive, and believed Jawaharlal's programme threatened private property, peaceful religious practices, and even personal safety. One of them described him as 'a wholehearted communist'; another declared that Jawaharlal was providing 'a through ticket to Moscow' (Chandra 1979: 187–9). The attacks of the industrialists did not deter Jawaharlal and he did not tone down his passion for socialism. He accused the twenty-one signatories of harbouring 'the fascist mentality' and reiterated his own sympathy for the underdog (JNSW: 7: 263, 280–4).

Jawaharlal lost the battle within the Congress, and this loss was related to an intervention by G.D. Birla, a prominent businessman. While Birla rebuked his capitalist colleagues for publicly condemning Jawaharlal's views on socialism, he hinted that it would help to strengthen the noble cause of property expropriation if pro-capitalist groups within the Congress—whom he identified as 'Mahatmaji's Group'—held office.

Birla argued that by publicly condemning Jawaharlal's views on socialism, the capitalists had brought shame upon themselves. To one of the signatories, Birla wrote:

'You have rendered no service to your caste men ... It looks very crude for a man with property to say that he is opposed to expropriation in the wider interests of the country'. He argued that those who have given up property should make the points against expropriation. The responsibility of capitalists lay in strengthening the hands of such people. He added that within the Congress, persons like Patel and Bhulabhai Desai were fighting socialism and the declaration of the capitalists had not helped people like Patel and Desai. Birla expected that those whom he identified as the 'Mahatmaji's Group' within the Congress would speak against socialism and for the interests of the capitalists. One way in which the latter could be served was by the acceptance of office by Congressmen and Birla was confident that '[t]he election which will take place will be controlled by [the] "Vallabhbhai Group" and if Lord Linlithgow handles the situation properly there is every likelihood of the Congressmen coming into office' (Mukherjee 2014:147).

There is evidence to suggest that Gandhi had assured Birla that the interests of the capitalists would be protected, and that Jawaharlal's commitment to socialism would have no practical implications. Birla, in a spirit of triumph, wrote to a fellow businessman: 'Mahatmaji kept his promise and without uttering a word, he saw that *no new commitments were made.*

Jawaharlalji's speech in a way was thrown into the waste paper basket because all the resolutions that were passed were against the spirit of his speech' (Mukherjee 2014: 148). Jawaharlal admitted to a friend: 'In the Working Committee meetings, I was completely isolated' (JNSW: 7: 214). Gandhi had thus outwitted Jawaharlal and undermined the latter's socialist vision and his opposition to office acceptance. Gandhi had first cornered Jawaharlal by having an important group in the Working Committee resign; he had then made his handpicked men to return, so that Jawaharlal was completely circumscribed in the Working Committee.

Jawaharlal was by no means unaware of what was happening and what he was up against. He wrote to Gandhi about his isolation, but appears to have accepted it without too many qualms. He could have resigned, but did not see himself—and did not want to be seen—as a quitter. The death of his father had also made him emotionally more dependent on Gandhi, and this was also a factor in Jawaharlal's decision to hang in there in spite of his ideological differences with senior members of the Working Committee. Jawaharlal's plight was aptly summed up by none other than G.D. Birla: 'He [Jawaharlal] could have caused a split by resigning but he did not ... Jawaharlalji seems to be like a typical English democrat who takes defeat in a sporting spirit. He seems to be out for giving expression to his ideology, but he realizes that action is impossible and so does not press for it' (Mukherjee 2014: 149).

Whatever his differences with some members of the Working Committee were and whatever misgivings he had about office acceptance, Jawaharlal's popularity had grown immensely. Forever the loyal Congressman, he campaigned enthusiastically in the days leading up to the elections. He travelled into the heart of rural India by train, car, bicycle, cart and steamer, and on camels, horses and elephants, and, of course, on foot. People thronged to hear him speak. Lal Bahadur Shastri, who was to succeed Jawaharlal as the prime minister of India, recalled how, on one occasion, the crowd was so large that Jawaharlal was compelled to walk on the shoulders of people and was later terribly ashamed that he had done so with his shoes on (Gopal: 1: 215). Jawaharlal was at the height of his popularity: the people of India seem to have discovered Jawaharlal Nehru.

While still in the din and bustle of the election campaign, Jawaharlal was re-elected as Congress president in December 1936 in Faizabad. Jawaharlal himself wanted the re-election. He explained to Gandhi that eight months was too short a term to revitalize the Congress, and that he wanted another term. His re-election was not without protests from some key players in the Congress. Patel wrote to Mahadev Desai, Gandhi's secretary, with a certain degree of venom that '[t]he decked-up groom-prince is ready to marry at one stroke as many girls as he can find'. Gandhi conveyed Patel's wish to Rajagopalachari that he, Rajagopalachari, take on the reins of the Congress. The latter declined, proposed the name of Govind Vallabh Pant, and added: 'As far as I am concerned, I would break loose and quit if he [Jawaharlal] continues'. Patel was willing to contest against Jawaharlal. It was only Gandhi's intervention that allowed Jawaharlal to enjoy a second term as the Congress president.

It would be simplistic to assume that Gandhi's support to Jawaharlal was based only on personal fondness. It was increasingly becoming evident that Jawaharlal was the rising new leader of the Congress, a distant second to Gandhi but nonetheless important. The Congress—to which Jawaharlal was bound by ties of loyalty and duty—had helped Jawaharlal come out of his cocoon-like existence: he had worked tirelessly for the party to become a front-rank leader. This position meant that the Congress, in turn, could not do without him. His Leftist orientation and the consequent hostility to the 'old guard' and the capitalists notwithstanding, he was indispensable to the party. His work during the election campaign only

41

underlined this point. Jawaharlal appealed to the youth and to the members of the Congress Socialist Party. His speeches and his intellectual orientation brought to these groups an international awareness, and also made them more sensitive to economic matters and how vital they were for India's freedom. He was also the Congress's best ambassador on international forums. Gandhi had unmatched charisma, but in his quiet way and relentless hard work, physical and intellectual, Jawaharlal had carved out a niche for himself within the Congress, and could not be ignored or sidelined. Above everything else, of course, he had Gandhi's support. Gandhi himself made this explicit in January1942: 'I have said for some years and say it now that not Rajaji, nor Sardar Vallabhbhai, but Jawaharlal will be my successor' (Gandhi 1991: 301).

In spite of Jawaharlal's unswerving loyalty to the Congress, there were two issues that deeply upset him. One was the decision of the Congress to accept office after its performance in the elections in which it had contested 1,161 of the 1,585 seats and had won 716. In six of the eleven provinces, it had a clear majority, while in three others, it was the single-largest party. Jawaharlal read the results as a clear indication of the prevalent anti-British spirit in India. But on office acceptance he found himself in a minority within the party. He argued that Congressmen were not out for the spoils of office but for attaining independence. On this, however, he was completely out of tune with the majority of Congressmen. Leaders like Rajagopalachari and Rajendra Prasad were in favour of accepting office; Patel acknowledged that given the mood of the Congress legislators and of the businessmen who had funded the elections, acceptance was very much on the cards. The Working Committee, in a bewildering compromise, authorized office acceptance but reiterated that the fundamental goal of the Congress was the destruction of the 1935 Act. Jawaharlal was devastated by the outcome and admitted to M.N. Roy, the communist leader, that he had been outwitted by Gandhi, who had accepted Jawaharlal's draft but had added a short supplementary paragraph that invalidated the rest of the resolution (Gopal: 1: 218–19).

The second issue that concerned Jawaharlal was the treatment meted out to his friend Subhas Chandra Bose by Gandhi and the 'old guard'. It is not as though Jawaharlal had no reservations about Bose: he was deeply uncomfortable with Bose's admiration for Mussolini and of Bose's handling of some of the affairs of the Congress in Bengal. Nonetheless, he was severely critical of the way the British government treated Bose—holding him without a specific charge against him. When the old guard of the Congress— Patel, Rajagopalachari, Pant, and others—conspired to make Bose's second term as president completely unworkable, Jawaharlal objected, even though privately he had advised Bose not to stand for a second term. He appealed to Gandhi to sit down with Bose to sort out the matter and to agree on a Working Committee. Gandhi refused to listen to Jawaharlal's pleas; Bose resigned as the president of the Congress at the end of April 1939. This set in motion a sequence of events that led to the exit of Bose from the Congress and the end of his friendship with Jawaharlal.

Thus when World War II broke out in September 1939, Jawaharlal found himself rather isolated and despondent within the Congress. He had intellectually foreseen that Europe was heading towards a major armed conflict and he also knew where his support was. He had always uncompromisingly been against fascism and Nazism. But unlike Gandhi, he could not offer unconditional co-operation to Britain. His hostility towards Hitler and Mussolini notwithstanding, Jawaharlal's response to the War was analytically more nuanced. He had argued that fascism and imperialism were interlinked, and opposed Chamberlain's appeasement policy. He wanted the Congress to adopt a similar position. After the outbreak of the War, Jawaharlal said in a speech: 'Only a free India can decide whether we can participate in the war or not. We want a declaration whether the principles of

44

democracy, liberty and self-determination for which the war is claimed to be fought will be applicable to India also ... A slave India cannot help Britain. We want to assume control of our government and when we are free we can help the democracies' (JNSW: 10: 184–5). The resolution of the Working Committee, which met over three days from 9 September, reflected upon the views of Jawaharlal, and postponed any decision till greater clarity was forthcoming from the government with regard to democracy and imperialism. At the suggestion of Gandhi, Jawaharlal wrote to Viceroy Lord Linlithgow in October 1939 that the War presented to Britain and India an opportunity to end the conflict between the two countries (JNSW: 10: 170–3). But the viceroy was unwilling to listen, and firmly turned down the idea of independence. Following this, the Working Committee asked the Congress ministers to resign.

An overture to a different kind of person on an equally important issue also ended in a stalemate. Jawaharlal wrote to Mohammad Ali Jinnah in October 1939, since the Muslim League was also committed to the idea of independence. He appealed to Jinnah to work with the Congress to ease the religious tension that existed between Hindus and Muslims, and offered any kind of help required. As a follow-up to this letter, Jawaharlal, Gandhi, and Prasad met

Jinnah in Delhi. Nothing substantial came out of the meeting, but Jawaharlal was optimistic. His hopes were dashed a month later, when Jinnah wrote to him to state that no understanding between the Congress and the Muslim League was possible 'so long as the Congress is not prepared to treat the Muslim League as the authoritative and representative organization of the Mussalmans of India'. Jawaharlal's reply to the letter was similarly forthright: 'If your desire is that we should consider the League as the sole organization representing the Muslims to the exclusion of all others, we are wholly unable to accede to it' (Nehru 1958: 414–15).

The failure of these negotiations left Jawaharlal feeling even more isolated and lonely. He poured his heart out to Gandhi: 'If I have to do anything worthwhile in life I must be true to myself insofar as I can. I have tried very hard to adapt myself to others, notably to you, but with little success, I fear. As for the Working Committee you know how badly I fit into it ... I function individually, lonely and weary at heart, disliking much that happens, including myself' (Iyengar and Zackariah 2011:378–9). Jawaharlal appeared to have cultivated a spirit of detachment, if not that of fatalism. He wrote on Christmas Day in 1939 to Madame Chiang Kai-Shek:'[F]or the present all of us have to go through the valley of the shadow' (JNSW: 10: 553–5).

His sense of isolation and despair was intensified by the Nazi–Soviet pact and the invasion of Finland by the Soviet Union. He had admired the Soviet Union for its principles and idealism, but now he saw that its choice of means to further its own interests was not above reproach. These events underlined for him the need for ethical action—this brought him closer to Gandhi. Jawaharlal took up spinning again in 1940 after a gap of four years.

By 1941, Jawaharlal's political and intellectual anguish was aggravated by the fact that he supported Britain's fight against Nazism but was opposed to Britain for its denial of independence for India. He expressed his dilemma to Rajendra Prasad: 'To say that Nazism is worse than the present form of British imperialism is true in some respects, though I doubt if there is fundamentally much difference. But to say that because Nazism is worse therefore we must prefer the domination of the British is surely [a] dangerous doctrine. It means that we are [a] helpless people who must have a master ...We stand for independence and we shall resist any and every foreign authority which seeks to dominate over us' (JNSW: 11: 33). Jawaharlal never retreated from this understanding as he watched the horrors of World War II unfold. He was also aware that the War would soon touch the borders of India. This awareness predicated a change in the position of the Congress. It was no longer possible to wait for a change in British policy. The Congress had to decide on what it would do if the Japanese invaded or bombed India. On this issue, a major difference arose between Jawaharlal and Gandhi. The former was ready to offer conditional support to the British in the fight against fascism. Within the Congress leadership, Jawaharlal was not alone in holding this view. Rajagopalachari and Maulana Abul Kalam Azad also held similar views. But predictably, Gandhi would not support any association with the War, as that would entail accepting violence. Gandhi had the support of Patel and Rajendra Prasad. Jawaharlal emphasized that the very special circumstances of the World War II would make it necessary for him to give up non-violence, which he had accepted when he entered politics.

These differences, however, were dissolved in the responses that the Congress leadership made to the Cripps Mission. Stafford Cripps, the Lord Privy Seal and an important member of the British war cabinet, arrived in India in March 1942 with a clutch of proposals aimed at pacifying the agitated nationalist mind in India. Cripps came to India with the promise of self-governance: India would be treated as a Dominion as a prelude to independence, which, in turn, would be preceded by a post–War Constituent Assembly. The immediate context of these proposals was to secure the co-operation of Indians in the War effort. Independence would be the reward for co-operation during the War. As Churchill commented at that time, '[w]e have resigned ourselves to fighting our utmost to defend India in order, if successful, to be turned out'. There seemed to be a strong element of insincerity in the proposals, and Cripps was chosen to provide them with credibility, since he had very good personal equations with both Gandhi and Jawaharlal.

However, the Cripps mission was ill-fated from the start. Immediately after meeting Cripps, Gandhi wrote to Jawaharlal: 'I am clearly of the view that we cannot accept the "offer"'. He famously described Cripps's offer as 'a post-dated cheque'. Jawaharlal was not as adversely disposed to Cripps's proposals as Gandhi was and it was generally believed that his views would be critical for the acceptance or the rejection of the Cripps offer. Jawaharlal believed that if the Congress could be part of a representative government under honourable terms, Indians could offer effective resistance to the Japanese. But the sticking point turned out to be how much say Indians would have in matters relating to defence. Churchill, Linlithgow, and Wavell, the commander-in-chief, were unwilling to yield, while the Congress, represented by Jawaharlal and Azad, demanded full responsibility for defence. Given this stand-off, the

Cripps offer, despite Cripps' and Jawaharlal's best intentions, was a dead letter.

Given his world view, Jawaharlal could not give up his opposition to Nazism and the Axis powers. But his views did not have support among Congressmen—including Gandhi—and among many Indians who were bitterly opposed to British rule. Thus Jawaharlal, once again, found himself isolated within his party. Additionally, while there was general agreement that the British should quit India, there was growing disagreement about what Indians should do in the event of a Japanese invasion of India—and such an invasion appeared imminent in 1941. Jawaharlal believed that the Japanese would have to be opposed, and even went to the extent of suggesting guerrilla warfare and a scorched earth policy. Gandhi argued that Indians had nothing against the Japanese and vice versa. He contemplated a mass civil disobedience movement against the British and even told Jawaharlal: 'If you won't join, I'll do it without you' (Gopal: 1: 292). As a last resort, the Congress made an appeal to the British government in mid-1942. It pleaded with the British to relinquish power because India's freedom was essential to ensure better conditions of resistance to the Japanese; the Congress did not want to embarrass the Allies in any way, but it also wanted the freedom of India. The Congress stated that if a withdrawal of the

British was not possible without preserving goodwill, the Congress would launch a non-violent movement under the leadership of Gandhi. Expecting a response, the Congress convened a meeting on 7 August 1942 to take a final decision. Both Gandhi and Jawaharlal felt that time had run out for more negotiations.

The British response came by way of an arrest of the entire Congress leadership on the early morning of 9 August, immediately after the Congress Working Committee passed the Quit India resolution. Thus began Jawaharlal's longest prison sentence—1,040 days, from 9 August 1942 to 15 June 1945. While he was in prison, India had erupted in popular violence against British rule—reminiscent of the revolt of 1857—and this had been brutally supressed. From 1942 until the end of the War, India had been virtually under military rule. Jawaharlal thus emerged from jail to a very different India. The nationalist movement was at its ebb. Collaborators of various kinds, including communists who had supported the British government during the war under the slogan 'People's War', thrived. Bengal lay ravaged by a famine that was the outcome of a deliberate policy directed by Churchill. Corruption and black marketeering were rampant. And there was in Wavell a new viceroy who propped up the Muslim League to unabashedly play the divide-and-rule card. He steadfastly refused to recognize the Congress as a non-Hindu secular organization, and echoed the views and sentiments of Jinnah. The elections to the central and provincial assemblies were held under these circumstances. The Congress organizational machinery was not quite prepared for the elections; Jawaharlal's own involvement in the election campaign in no way matched the vigour he had displayed ten years ago. The Muslim League improved its position. Jawaharlal, however, tended to underestimate the gains of the League, and believed that so long as the British remained in India, there would be no solution to the communal problem.

Jawaharlal's attention was drawn at this time to the plight of the soldiers of the Indian National Army, who were being tried as traitors by the British government. He met these prisoners, and from the conversations he had with them, he radically altered his views about Subhas Bose's role in Southeast Asia. He organized relief for the Indian National Army prisoners, championed their cause, and even donned his barrister's gown after twenty-five years to appear in their defence. The other issue that concerned him, once dear to his heart, was the condition of Asia in the aftermath of the War. He wanted to visit Burma, Malaya, and Indonesia, and welcomed the idea of an Asian conference proposed by Aung San of Burma. He travelled to Singapore and Malaya, halting briefly in Rangoon, Burma, to meet Aung San. This was a great show of solidarity on

Jawaharlal's part towards other Asian countries that had suffered under foreign domination.

Such issues, however, became peripheral with the rise of popular discontent against the Raj in India. In early 1946, the Royal Air Force mutinied at many stations in India: they were angry at the terms of demobilization and their pay. Some members of the Royal Indian Air Force even went on a hunger strike. Much more serious was the naval mutiny in Bombay, in which 3,000 ratings of the Royal Indian Navy hoisted their national flag on their ships and staged a demonstration through the streets of Bombay. Industrial workers went on strike in sympathy, and there was an exchange of fire between British troops and the mutineers. The city of Bombay had never seen such a disturbance. Echoing the priorities of the government, Patel and others of the old guard in the Congress wanted the mutineers to stop their resistance. Jawaharlal went to Bombay, much to Patel's displeasure. Jawaharlal pleaded with the sailors to call off their action since they had no chance of success. The mutiny stopped. But these were seven days that shook Bombay, the British government, and the Congress.

It was increasing becoming clear to the Congress leadership, including Jawaharlal, that there were forces at work in India which the Congress could no longer control. The British, in turn, were convinced that the very basis of their rule was becoming untenable. Churchill's successor as prime minister, Clement Attlee, decided to send out a team of three cabinet ministers to discuss India's freedom and transfer of power. This team—the Cabinet Mission as it came to be called—was composed of Cripps, Pethick-Lawrence, and A. V. Alexander. Jawaharlal's own attitude to the Cabinet Mission was clear: the independence of India only would serve as the basis of all parleys and negotiations. Any discussion on Dominion Status was irrelevant; the situation had altered dramatically since Cripps's last visit. He believed that the future of independent India would be a Constituent Assembly, formed of delegates elected by provincial assemblies according to proportional representation. Even the question of Pakistan should be left to be decided by the Constituent Assembly.

But the reality of negotiations turned out to be more complex. Predictably, the Congress and the Muslim League could agree on very little. As a first move, the Cabinet Mission put out on 8 May 1946 a proposal titled *Suggested Points for Agreement* between the Congress and the League. This document said that there should be an all-India government and provincial legislature, both having equal proportions from the Hindu-majority and the Muslim-majority provinces. The all-India government would deal with foreign affairs, defence, communications, and fundamental rights. Residuary powers would rest with the provinces, and groups of provinces could be formed. The fact that the Mission did not insist on groups was seen by the viceroy as a concession to the Congress, and Jinnah sang the same tune. With no agreement reached, the Mission issued its own plan on 16 May. This plan rejected partition in any form. The all-India government would handle foreign policy, defence, communications, and finance. All other matters were to be with the provinces. On any major communal problem, it was laid down that the majority of each community would be a requirement as well as an overall majority. Jawaharlal was impatient with the working out of these details: he was eager to arrive at a settlement on the basis of independence at once.

The Cabinet Mission's plan contained the seeds of future trouble. The League accepted the plan, interpreting it to mean that grouping was compulsory. But Gandhi and Azad were separately assured that grouping was not compulsory. With the promise of an interim government in the near future, Jawaharlal took over the reins of the Congress presidency from Azad. The former convened a meeting of the All India Congress Committee in Bombay, where (and at a press conference a few days later) Jawaharlal spoke explicitly against grouping, emphasizing the fact that it was not compulsory as per the plan. This rather scattered Jinnah's pigeons. Jinnah immediately withdrew the League's acceptance of the Cabinet Mission's plan, arguing that the interpretation that the Congress had made of the plan had freed the League from its own promise. At that point of time, it seemed to some, most importantly to Azad and Patel, that an important opportunity had been lost. The Muslim League (read: Jinnah) for once had agreed to something but Jawaharlal's announcement had only served to return Jinnah to his obstructionist ways. This, according to Jawaharlal's later-day critics, had made partition inevitable.

This controversy—a storm in a teacup given the way events unfolded—needs to be put into context. The ambiguity regarding grouping was embedded in the Mission's plan; it would not even be unfair to suggest, given the overall thrust of British policy at that time, that it deliberately played both ends against the middle, promising the League one thing and to the Congress its exact opposite. From Jawaharlal's point of view, it could be said that he had done and said nothing that was inconsistent with the Congress's policies. He wanted to make it abundantly clear to the British, especially at this juncture, that the Congress wanted India to act and function as an independent sovereign state. The conjuncture was important since Jinnah was aware that the Mission was not accepting his most important demand—partition. Most importantly, given

Jinnah's track record, there was no guarantee that he would stand by his acceptance of the Cabinet Mission plan, which put him at a serious disadvantage. He had merely seized the first available opportunity. It is not unreasonable to argue that he would have got out in any case then or a little later.

The Great Calcutta Killing, the direct outcome of Jinnah's Direct Action Day on 16 August 1946, made any prospect of a settlement with the Muslim League virtually impossible. Jawaharlal wrote to Wavell, the then viceroy, '… we are not going to shake hands with murder or allow it to determine the country's policy' (Gopal: 1: 331). Wavell, very reluctantly, had to proceed with the formation of an interim government, and on 2 September, what the Congress liked to regard as a provisional national government was sworn in. Jawaharlal became the vice-president of the Executive Council and held the portfolios of external affairs and Commonwealth relations. Immediately after the swearing in of this government, Jawaharlal wrote, 'Too long have we been passive spectators of events, the playthings of others. The initiative comes to our people now and we shall make the history of our choice'. Wavell continued with his efforts to get the Muslim League to join the government, which it did in October 1946, but the League members worked to obstruct the functioning of the government.

Matters, however, were put on a fast track with an announcement from Prime Minister Clement Attlee that the British would withdraw from India no later than June 1948. This made it obvious that the work of the Constituent Assembly, which had met for the first time on 9 December 1946 but had been adjourned repeatedly, could no longer be deferred.

By this time, driven to despair by Jinnah's intransigence and propensity for going back on promises and agreements, both the British government and the Congress leadership (except Gandhi) had accepted that there was no way forward save accepting Jinnah's demand for Pakistan in one form or another. A large part of the negotiations of what the British came to call 'Transfer of Power' was concerned with what form Partition would take. Jawaharlal continued to cling to an illusory hope. In April 1947, he wrote, 'I have no doubt whatever that sooner or later India will have to function as a unified country. Perhaps the best way to reach that stage is to go through some kind of partition now' (Gopal: 1: 343). He also reposed trust in Lord Mountbatten, who had arrived as the viceroy in March 1947. Jawaharlal relied on Mountbatten to work out a viable plan for partitioning India. This trust could produce moments of high drama.

On the night of 10 May 1947, when Jawaharlal was Mountbatten's guest in Simla, the latter showed him the full text of a proposal called 'Plan Balkan', which the British cabinet had already approved. By this proposal, power would be demitted to the provinces and they would be left to decide whether they would join to form any groups. Most of the important features of the plan were new to Jawaharlal, and by Mountbatten's own evidence, he was furious. The following morning, Jawaharlal wrote to Mountbatten rejecting Plan Balkan: 'The whole approach was completely different from what ours had been, and the picture of India that emerged frightened me ... a picture of fragmentation and conflict and disorder ...' (Ziegler 1985: 379). Jawaharlal was willing to accept partition as an unavoidable evil, but unwilling to countenance a proposal that broke up India into pieces. Mountbatten was forced to go back to the drawing board. A new plan was drawn up by which Punjab and Bengal would be partitioned if the Muslim-majority districts or the rest of the province wanted it; Sind could decide through its assembly which state it wanted to join; the plan would not affect the princes; and the North West Frontier Province would be part of Pakistan. Jawaharlal and his colleagues approved of this plan and wanted it to be implemented as soon as possible, as violence had already broken out in Punjab and Bengal.

The transfer of power negotiations took place under the shadow of communal violence. As Jawaharlal wrote to Sarvepalli Radhakrishnan, '[w]e are at present living in the midst of crises and the situation is volcanic ...' (Gopal: 1: 352). These circumstances must have forced the hands of Jawaharlal and the other Congress leaders, so much so that they collectively chose to disregard the views and sentiments of Gandhi. India gained independence by betraying one of the principal pillars of the Indian national movement, that India was one, united country. In the euphoria of independence, nobody except Gandhi quite foresaw what the immediate future was to bring.

3

The Mahatma's Disciple

It could not have been easy for Jawaharlal to go against the explicit wishes of Gandhi on as critical an issue as the partition of India. Gandhi made his sadness and his disapproval evident by not being present in Delhi during the celebrations on 15 August 1947. He stayed in Beliaghata in east Calcutta, declaring the day to be one for fasting and prayer. The Father of the Nation made his point by being absent at the birth of the nation. His absence was perhaps felt most sharply by Jawaharlal, his foremost disciple and chosen heir. Their relationship had been very close, but it had not always been a smooth relationship. There had been too many differences—the one on Partition being the last. Within five-and-a-half months of India gaining independence, Gandhi was assassinated by a Hindu fanatic. On getting the news of the murder, Jawaharlal had rushed to Birla

House, where, upon seeing Gandhi's lifeless body, he sobbed like a child (Gopal: 2: 25). But the differences never diminished the personal bond.

Jawaharlal first met Gandhi in 1915, around the time of the Lucknow Congress session, and it was certainly not love at first sight. Gandhi had returned to India from South Africa in 1914 and was entering Indian politics. Jawaharlal found Gandhi to be different from other political leaders, but he also appeared to young Jawaharlal as distant and unpolitical (A: 35). There is no record of Gandhi's reaction, if any, to this meeting. This absence of any recorded reaction may have been related to Jawaharlal's attitude. Jawaharlal was also, in this phase of his life, contemptuous of the Indian National Congress. He had gone to the 1912 Congress session at Bankipore and had found it 'very much an English-knowing upper-class affair where morning coats and well-pressed trousers were greatly in evidence. Essentially it was a social gathering with no political excitement or tension' (A: 27).

This ambience of the Congress was poised to change under the influence of Gandhi. Jawaharlal recorded how Gandhi's 'adventures and victory in Champaran, on behalf of the tenants of the planters filled us with enthusiasm' (A: 35). Even this enthusiasm has to be read in the context of Jawaharlal's use of the word 'adventures'; he was not willing to see the *satyagraha* in Champaran as a full-blown protest with enduring implications. This attitude, too, changed dramatically when Gandhi launched the Rowlatt Satyagraha in 1919. Jawaharlal, in his own words, was 'afire with enthusiasm' because he saw in the movement 'a way out of the tangle, a method of action which was straight and open and possibly effective' (A: 41). He wanted to join the protests immediately. He wrote later, 'I hardly thought of the consequences—law-breaking, gaol-going, etc.—and if I thought of them I did not care'. Jawaharlal's father, however, was not as enthusiastic; he seems to have convinced Gandhi to dissuade Jawaharlal from joining the movement, which would lead the latter to jail. If one was to go by Jawaharlal's autobiography, this was his first important encounter with Gandhi and he was not happy with the outcome since Gandhi advised him 'not to precipitate matters or to do anything which might upset father'. So his father and the future father figure tempered Jawaharlal's enthusiasm to jump into the nationalist movement. Jawaharlal yielded to Gandhi's advice in spite of his own feelings.

This was the first piece in what would emerge as a pattern. The term *future father figure* is used deliberately because in the very first letter Jawaharlal wrote to Gandhi on 12 March 1924—the first in a stream of correspondence that lasted till Gandhi's death—he

addressed Gandhi as 'My dear Bapuji' and signed off
'Yours affectionately'. There were no formalities, and
the ties of affection were apparent. These ties were
the outcome of Jawaharlal's immersion in the Non-
Cooperation Movement that Gandhi launched in
1920. He recalled in his autobiography how he had
become 'wholly absorbed in the movement ... [giving]
up all my other associations and contacts, old friends,
books, even newspapers ... In spite of the strength
of my family bonds, I almost forgot my family, my
wife, my daughter' (A: 77). He wrote that working
for the Non-Cooperation Movement in 1921 under
Gandhi's leadership was like living through 'a kind of
intoxication'. There was 'excitement and optimism and
a buoyant enthusiasm' (A: 69). All this notwithstanding,
he had his doubts. He was worried about the emergence
of religious feelings in Indian politics, among both
Hindus and Muslims. He believed that these religious
feelings obfuscated thought. Jawaharlal often found
himself being out of tune with some of Gandhi's
phrases, especially his frequent references to *Ram Rajya*
as a golden age that would return. Jawaharlal admitted
to himself that Gandhi's language was difficult to
comprehend for the average modern person. But he
was convinced that Gandhi was 'a great and unique
man and a glorious leader', and was willing to write
for Gandhi 'an almost blank cheque for the time being

at least' (A: 72–3). Jawaharlal's allegiance to Gandhi and his doctrine of non-violence was almost unqualified at this stage in his life, but not without doubts and queries.

If Jawaharlal had his doubts about Gandhi's message, the latter used his influence to rein in Jawaharlal's growing radicalism. This radicalism was leavened by what he had seen in Europe during his visit in 1926. He was already leaning towards socialism. Jawaharlal noted this transformation: 'My outlook was wider, and nationalism by itself seemed to me definitely a narrow and insufficient creed. Political freedom, independence, were no doubt essential, but they were steps only in the right direction; without social freedom and a socialistic structure of society and the State, neither the country nor the individual could develop much' (A: 166). In keeping with this new-found radicalism, Jawaharlal felt that Congress should commit itself to the goal of independence. At the Madras Congress session in 1927, he had a resolution passed declaring 'the goal of the Indian people to be complete independence' (JNSW: 3: 5).

Gandhi commented on the resolution in Young India that 'we [the Congress] have almost sunk to the level of the schoolboys' debating society', and described the resolution demanding independence to be a 'tragedy' (CWMG: 35: 456). Gandhi also condemned the resolution as being 'hastily conceived' and 'thoughtlessly passed' (CWMG: 35: 438). He warned Jawaharlal, 'You are going too fast. You should have taken time to think. Most of the resolutions you framed and got carried could have been delayed for one year' (Iyengar and Zackariah 2011: 44). Jawaharlal resented these comments from Gandhi, and was very forthright in his reply: 'It passes my comprehension how a national organization can have as its ideal and goal Dominion Status. The very idea suffocates and strangles me' (Iyengar and Zackariah 2011: 48). Jawaharlal used the occasion to express to Gandhi for the first time his fundamental differences with some of Gandhi's views and opinions. He wrote that while he admired Gandhi and believed in him as 'a leader who can lead this country to victory and freedom',

[He] hardly agreed with anything that some of your previous publications—Indian Home Rule, etc.—contained. I felt and feel that you were and are infinitely greater than your little books ... And I felt instinctively that however much I may disagree with you, your great personality and your possession of these qualities ["action and daring and courage"] would carry us to our goal.

Jawaharlal told Gandhi that 'during the non-cooperation period you were supreme' but since

Gandhi had come out of prison, he had changed, and had been 'very obviously ill at ease'. Jawaharlal, like many others, had been bewildered by this and Gandhi's proneness to changing his attitude at short notice. Jawaharlal went on to express his reservations about Gandhi's emphasis on *khadi*; Jawaharlal wrote, 'I do not see how freedom is coming in its [khadi's] train.' According to Jawaharlal, Gandhi offered no way forward but only criticized. Jawaharlal continued in this letter to spell out his deeper differences with Gandhi:

Reading many of your articles in *Young India*—your autobiography, etc.—I have often felt how very different my ideals were from yours. And I have felt that you were very hasty in your judgements, or rather having arrived at certain conclusions you were over eager to justify them by any scrap of evidence you might get ... You misjudge greatly I think the civilization of the West and attach too great an importance to its many failings. You have stated somewhere that India has nothing to learn from the West and that she has reached a pinnacle of wisdom in the past. I entirely disagree with this viewpoint and I neither think that the so-called *Rama Raj* was very good in the past, nor do I want it back. I think the western or industrial civilization is bound to conquer India, maybe with many changes and adaptations, but nonetheless in the main based on industrialism. You have criticised strongly the many obvious defects of industrialism and hardly paid any attention to its merits. Everyone knows these defects ... It is the opinion of most thinkers in the West that these defects are not due to industrialism as such but to the capitalist system which is based on the exploitation of others. I believe you have stated that in your opinion there is no necessary conflict between Capital and Labour. I think that under the capitalist system this conflict is unavoidable. (Iyengar and Zackariah 2011: 50–2)

Gandhi did not directly address the issues Jawaharlal raised. Instead, he wrote, he was relieved that Jawaharlal had been released from 'self-suppression' and had been able to articulate his differences. He added:

I see quite clearly that you must carry on open warfare against me and my views ... The differences between you and me appear so vast and radical that there seems to be no meeting ground between us. I can't conceal from you my grief that I should lose a comrade so valiant, so faithful, so able and so honest as you have always been....

But he hoped that in spite of 'grave political differences', Jawaharlal and he would continue their personal intimacy (Iyengar and Zackariah 2011: 56). Jawaharlal was pained by this response from Gandhi and confessed that he had not 'thought of the possibility of any warfare between you and me'. He told Gandhi, 'No one has moved me and inspired me more than you and I can never forget your exceeding kindness to me', and proceeded to ask him, 'am I not your child in politics, though perhaps a truant and errant child?' (Iyengar and Zackariah 2011: 57–8).

Unwittingly, Jawaharlal had taken the first steps towards setting a pattern for the future with regard to his relationship with Gandhi. Time and again Jawaharlal would express in clear terms his differences with Gandhi—on occasion, such expressions would border on defiance or even rebellion—but would pull back after remembering his ties of affection with Gandhi and his recognition of the unique position that Gandhi enjoyed in the Indian national movement. As Subhas Bose once correctly noted, 'His [Jawaharlal's] head pulls one way and his heart in another direction. His heart is with Gandhi' (Mukherjee 2014: 105). In his turn, Gandhi was patient with Jawaharlal's periodic outbursts. He was fond of Jawaharlal, and recognized and valued the latter's dependence on him especially after the death of Motilal Nehru. At the end of 1946, Gandhi wrote to Jawaharlal, 'I claim to be like a wise father to you, having no less love towards you than Motilalji'. He described Jawaharlal's affection for him to be 'extraordinary and so natural!' (Iyengar and Zackariah 2011: 471).

The twin pulls of difference and dependence surfaced most poignantly in Jawaharlal's reactions in the aftermath of the Gandhi–Irwin Pact, Gandhi's fast and the withdrawal of the Civil Disobedience movement. In his autobiography, Jawaharlal recalled his mood of disillusionment and resignation when he learnt of the Gandhi–Irwin Pact in March 1931. He remembered how, on that March night, he had asked himself, 'Was it for this that our people had behaved so gallantly for a year? Were all our brave words and deeds to end in this?' And he summed up his mood with the famous lines from T.S. Eliot: 'This is the way the world ends,/Not with a bang, but a whimper' (A: 259). He took his feelings to Gandhi the day after the pact had been signed and found Gandhi's justification of the pact 'to be a forced one, and I was not convinced, but I was somewhat soothed by his talk' (A: 260). But all his reservations evaporated when he heard in prison that Gandhi had begun a fast unto death in January 1932 to protest against Ramsay MacDonald's proposal to have separate electorates for the 'Depressed Classes'. He recorded in his prison diary, 'I cried and wept' (JNSW: 5: 408). He was distraught that Gandhi had chosen a side issue for 'his final sacrifice' (JNSW: 5: 407), and was confused about what this meant for the freedom movement. These political considerations were, however, set aside by his sense of personal loss. He wrote to his daughter, Indira, 'I am shaken up completely and

I know not what to do. News has come, terrible news, that Bapu has determined to starve himself to death. My little world in which he has occupied such a big place shakes and totters, and there seems to be darkness and emptiness everywhere ... Shall I not see him again? And whom shall I go to when I am in doubt and require wise counsel, or am afflicted and in sorrow and need loving comfort' (GWH: 379). Overcoming his personal feelings, Jawaharlal sent a telegram expressing his agony to Gandhi, but ended it with the words, '[H]ow can I presume to advise a magician[?]' (Iyengar and Zackariah 2011: 168). By using the word 'magician', Jawaharlal was perhaps admitting that Gandhi had that rare gift of feeling the mood of the people and leading them in a campaign.

Similar sentiments of despair and disappointment overwhelmed him when in prison in 1933, he heard that Gandhi had withdrawn the Civil Disobedience movement. He experienced an inner emptiness and felt frightened by Gandhi's statement that Congressmen should turn to social work. 'A vast distance', he wrote, 'seemed to separate him [Gandhi] from me. With a stab of pain I felt that the chords of allegiance that had bound me to him for many years had snapped' (A: 506). About a month after Gandhi began his self-purificatory fast on 8 May 1933, Jawaharlal noted in his prison diary:

As I watched the emotional upheaval during the fast I wondered more and more if this was the right method in politics. It is sheer revivalism and clear thinking has not a ghost of a chance against it ... I am afraid I am drifting further and further away from him mentally, in spite of my strong emotional attachment to him. (JNSW: 5: 478)

A month later, his noting in his diary was more definitive: 'I am getting more and more certain that there can be no further political cooperation between Bapu and me. At least not of the kind that has existed. We had better go our different ways' (JNSW: 5: 489). The break never came, and the first diary entry (quoted above) provides a clue to understanding why it never happened. Jawaharlal wrote about his 'strong emotional attachment' to Gandhi. That this sentiment was reciprocated is revealed by the letter Gandhi wrote to Jawaharlal as he commenced his fast:

As I was struggling against the coming fast, you were before me as it were in flesh and blood ... How I wish I could feel that you had understood the absolute necessity of it. The Harijan movement is too big for mere intellectual effort. There is nothing so bad in all the world. And yet I cannot leave religion and therefore Hinduism. My religion would be a burden to me, if Hinduism failed me. I love Christianity, Islam and many other faiths through Hinduism. Take it away and nothing remains for me. But then I cannot tolerate it with untouchability ... But I won't convince you by argument, if you did not see the truth intuitively. I know that even if I do not carry your approval with me, I shall retain your precious love during all those days of ordeal. (Iyengar and Zackariah 2011: 180)

Jawaharlal was deeply touched by this letter and described as a 'typical cry from the heart' and responded to it thus by telegram: 'What can I say about matters I do not understand. I feel lost in strange country where you are only familiar landmark and I try to grope my way in dark but I stumble' (Iyengar and Zackariah 2011: 181).

These expressions of difference remained the subject of discussion and debate between Jawaharlal and Gandhi. But it was not in the nature of either individual to keep such fundamental differences only in the private domain: Gandhi was Jawaharlal's personal anchor. Jawaharlal stated his position in his autobiography when he wrote that he considered Gandhi's views, as presented in *Hind Swaraj*, to be

[an] utterly wrong and harmful doctrine, and impossible of achievement ... This desire to get away from the mind of man to primitive conditions where mind does not count, seems to me quite incomprehensible.

The very thing that is the glory and triumph of man is decried and discouraged, and a physical environment which will oppress the mind and prevent is growth is considered desirable. Present-day civilization is full of evils, but it is also full of good: and it has the capacity in it to rid itself of those evils. To destroy it root and branch is to remove that capacity from it and revert to a dull, sunless and miserable existence. (A: 510–11)

Gandhi never resented the expression of these differences; neither did these expressions prevent him from declaring on 15 January 1942 that Jawaharlal was his chosen heir. On that day at the All India Congress Committee session in Wardha, Gandhi said:

Somebody suggested that Pandit Jawaharlal and I were estranged. It will require much more than differences of opinion to estrange us. We have had differences from the moment we became co-workers, yet I have said for some years and say it now that not Rajaji, nor Sardar Vallabhbhai, but Jawaharlal will be my successor. You cannot divide water by repeatedly striking it with a stick. It is just as difficult to divide us ... when I am gone, he will speak my language. (CWMG: 75: 224)

Certain personal factors influenced the choice. These are revealed in what Vallabhbhai Patel wrote to Jawaharlal on 3 July 1939: 'I don't think that he loves

74

anybody more than he loves you and when he finds that any action of his has made you unhappy he broods over it and feels miserable' (Nehru Papers: vol. 81).

4

As Prime Minister

In his very first speech as the prime minister of India, Jawaharlal had coined a phrase that became an integral part of India's national lexicon: 'Years ago we made a *tryst with destiny*' (emphasis mine). The use of that pronoun 'we' would come to haunt him at least in the very first few months of his premiership. Whom had he spoken for? Tens of thousands of people in the divided provinces of Punjab and Bengal were uprooted by the partition that came with independence. Had he spoken for them? Jawaharlal perhaps underestimated the emotional upheaval that the Partition had brought in the lives of people. Ignoring the trauma, he saw the violence that ensued in terms of groups of individuals who had lost their reason: 'There is madness about in its worst form', he wrote to Lady Ismay a fortnight or so after 15 August. But he was honest enough to admit, at least privately, that all his calculations when he had agreed to the Partition as a way of ending communal violence had proved to be utterly misplaced (Gopal: 2: 13–14). Jawaharlal was also aware that he had a responsibility to his countrymen in spite of his growing sense of helplessness. He had to begin the process of building anew from the remains of devastation.

Jawaharlal chose to lead by example. He moved around Delhi trying to reassure Muslim families, and occasionally jumping into mobs to quell the violence that emanated from fanaticism and a sense of victimhood. He wanted to clear the air of panic and fear. He addressed public meetings in northern India and made broadcasts to maintain peace and to adhere to the principles of religious tolerance, which was the bedrock of the Constitution. In a speech at Allahabad in December 1947, he said, 'The battle of our political freedom is fought and won. But another battle, no less important than what we have won, still faces us. It is a battle with no outside enemy ... It is a battle with our own selves'. That internal battle entailed not just quelling frenzied mobs on the streets, but also in persuading some members of his own cabinet that, as the prime minister of India, he could not merely speak for and protect the interests of the Hindu majority. This attitude naturally found a profound resonance in Gandhi, who, back in Delhi from Bengal and Calcutta in September, supported Nehru's efforts to protect the minorities and to abjure the sentiments of retaliation. While Gandhi offered moral support and inspiration, Mountbatten, now in his incarnation as the first governor-general of India, lent Jawaharlal support in administrative matters. The administrative problem was much more than preventing the escalation of violence, even though that was the priority of the moment. Of equal importance was setting up relief camps and hospitals, and establishing administrative procedures and policy frameworks, especially with regard to Pakistan. To make matters worse for Jawaharlal, as he became involved in these complex issues, the problem over Kashmir erupted (this is addressed later in a separate section in this chapter).

Partition, communal violence, administrative matters, policymaking, and all other issues relating to governance were, of course, waylaid by the numbing assassination of Gandhi at the end of January 1948. Jawaharlal's prime ministership was thus born under the sign of tragedy: violence, confusion, and a profound personal loss. Jawaharlal must have felt in those early months like a soul tied upon a wheel of fire.

Early Years

Even in the very early days of his tenure, Jawaharlal felt frustrated, depressed, and alienated by the factionalism, fight for office, and a pronounced Hindu tilt within the Congress, including among some of the leaders. He looked around for people who would support him to build a new kind of India. With this in mind, he persuaded Rajagopalachari to come to Delhi as the successor to Mountbatten. He had had differences in the past with Rajagopalachari, but believed that the two of them were in agreement on basic factors: one major area of concurrence was their belief that minorities should be treated with care and sensitivity. Rajagopalachari's support here was critical to Jawaharlal to counterbalance the views of Patel, who, together with a large body of Congressmen, was beginning to represent an orthodox Hindu opinion. Jawaharlal's relationship with Rajagopalachari blossomed, and he wanted the latter to continue as the first president of the Indian republic. This was not to be: Congressmen preferred Rajendra Prasad, who had served as the president of the Constituent Assembly as the head of the Indian state. Jawaharlal tried to influence Prasad to declare that he was not interested in the high office and to propose the name of Rajagopalachari. Prasad was not willing to do this. Jawaharlal discovered that Patel wanted Prasad in office and had been mobilizing support for his candidature within the Congress. Jawaharlal had no other alternative but to accept defeat.

Thus, the Republic of India began its journey with the first prime minister burdened with a president whom he did not like, and with whom he had many fundamental differences of outlook and values. The nature of these differences was evident when Prasad objected on astrological grounds to 26 January 1950 as the date for inaugurating the Republic. Jawaharlal would have none of this and chose to overrule the president-elect.

In these early years as prime minister, Jawaharlal had to be involved with the making of the Constitution as well. He drafted and proposed the Objectives Resolution that would make India a sovereign republic with a constitution that guaranteed fundamental liberties and justice for all, and ensured that there would be adequate safeguards for the minorities and the tribals. He worked to make it possible for the Constitution to create a parliamentary democracy. There were some areas in which he had more success than in others. He curbed the enthusiasm for Hindi and made English as an official language at least till 1965. He spoke for and with the majority in rejecting proportional representation. He favoured the idea of amending the Constitution through a simple majority in parliament, but stopped short of moving an amendment to this effect. On some other rather important issues, Jawaharlal could not have his way. Patel proposed that Privy Purses, which had been promised to the princes as the price for accession, should be guaranteed to them for perpetuity under the

Constitution. Jawaharlal considered this to be wasteful public expenditure, but found no effective way to counter Patel. Another issue on which Jawaharlal had to give in was on the right of property as a fundamental right. He was opposed to the idea. A more complicated issue that arose from the recognition of the right to property was in regards to compensation in case of expropriation of private property. Patel believed that a just and equitable compensation followed logically from the right to property. Jawaharlal had no principled objection to the principle of compensation, but since he was pushing the issue of abolition of *zamindari*, he wanted to make it clear that the legislature, not the courts, should decide what principle the compensation would be paid on. But in no way did this remove the issue of compensation from judicial scrutiny. Jawaharlal wanted a ceiling on compensation and to bring it out of the courts' jurisdiction. The Supreme Court did not agree with this, and in 1955, at Jawaharlal's insistence, the Constitution was amended to debar the courts from looking into the question of compensation.

Thus, Jawaharlal was not in a particularly happy frame of mind as he embarked on his career as India's first prime minister. The many problems that he faced were compounded by an insurgency led by the communists, who believed that India's independence was a fake one. As Jawaharlal looked around, he was saddened by what he thought was a fall in standards. India was on the brink of a new era, but Jawaharlal felt that the resolve and confidence required to push forward the new era were missing. He despaired that India was in a kind of ideological vacuum. Writing to his chief ministers in February 1950, he commented: 'We talk of capitalism and socialism and communism, and yet we lack the social content of all of these'. He felt isolated and lonely. Jawaharlal expressed his sense of isolation to Patel, his principal political opponent within the government: 'I see every ideal that I have held fading away and conditions emerging in India which not only distress me but indicate to me that my life's work has been a failure' (Gopal: 2: 87). He was especially upset by his inability to reach out to the political leadership in Pakistan to work together to address the problem of refugees and minorities, in both India and Pakistan. He wrote to President Rajendra Prasad in March 1950, expressing his desire to resign. This was not an empty expression of despair: Jawaharlal even wrote to some of his senior colleagues, urging them not to resign following his resignation. But he abandoned the idea of resigning, as he realized that by resigning, he would only play into the hands of his opponents and critics who wanted him out of office.

Putting aside his personal feelings, he decided to reach out one more time to Liaquat Ali Khan to forge an agreement in regards to the treatment of minorities. This time he managed to secure an agreement, even though the meeting lasted a week and eleven drafts were needed. What brought India and Pakistan together was the desire on both sides to avoid a war. By the agreement, signed in April 1950, both governments bound themselves to ensure equality to minorities. Once the pact was sealed, the person who worked tirelessly to implement it on the India side was, much to Jawaharlal's surprise and admiration, Patel. Jawaharlal noted this in a very characteristic English turn of phrase: 'Vallabhbhai', he wrote to Rajagopalachari, 'has been a brick during these days'. Not unexpectedly, the pact collapsed on the Pakistan side no sooner than it had been signed.

In these early years of independent India, Jawaharlal had also to sort out matters within the Congress. The party had lost much of the idealism that had driven it in the high noon of Indian nationalism. 'We have lost something', Jawaharlal wrote in July 1950, 'the spirit that moves and unless we recapture that spirit, all our labour will yield little profit.' What irked him most was the attitude of some prominent leaders like Purushottam Das Tandon, the president of the Uttar Pradesh Provincial Congress, and even Patel and Pant on occasion, towards the Muslims and towards Hindu communalism. Jawaharlal decided to move, and the election for Congress president in August 1950 provided him the opportunity. He opposed the candidacy of Tandon and made his views public, even though he was aware that Tandon had the support of Patel, Pant, and the Uttar Pradesh ministry. He informed Patel that he would find it impossible to continue in the Working Committee if Tandon was to be elected. Tandon's victory seemed to his opponents to be the perfect chance to clip Jawaharlal's wings. But they reckoned without his political skills. Jawaharlal refused to serve on the Working Committee, and through powerful speeches, he made Congress bodies accept resolutions that articulated his viewpoint. He also considered removing Patel from the States ministry, but he did not carry the idea through, as he got to know that Patel was terminally ill. Jawaharlal was persuaded to remain in the Working Committee, but he expressed his disapproval of many other members that Tandon had selected, and retained the right to raise fundamental issues at the first meeting of the new Committee. Jawaharlal was taking the first steps to have the Congress aligned to his way of thinking. The bickering with Tandon continued, and this wearied Jawaharlal. He finally resigned from the Working Committee in August 1951, making it clear that he would brook no compromise, since the differences were matters of basic policy.

'Which viewpoint and outlook are to prevail in the Congress—Tandon's or mine? It is on this issue that a clear decision should be arrived at and any attempt to shirk it will simply mean that the issue will arise every month in an acuter form', Jawaharlal declared to B.C. Roy. Matters came to a head in the AIIC meeting in early September, Tandon resigned, and Jawaharlal was elected president of the Congress—he was now the head of the party and the government. In a speech in Delhi in October 1951, Jawaharlal made his opinions and intentions abundantly clear: 'If any person raises his hand to strike down another on the ground of religion, I shall fight him till the last breath of my life, both as the head of the government and from outside' (Gopal: 2: 155).

It was important for the Congress and for Jawaharlal that the latter be in command as the first general elections were around the corner. The elections would be held on universal adult suffrage. Jawaharlal was not unaware of the problems of holding elections on universal adult suffrage in a country with a huge poor and illiterate population. But this was an act of faith on Jawaharlal's part and a public expression of his unalloyed commitment to democracy in India. As in his fight against communal elements, here too, Jawaharlal would not accept any compromise. The election was a massive administrative exercise, in which, under the leadership of Sukumar Sen, the chief election officer, a million officials were involved. A hundred seventy-three million voters were registered through house-to-house surveys. Around 75 per cent of people entitled to vote could not read and write, and procedures had to be devised to overcome this drawback. Elections were spread over 3,772 constituencies and held over six months from October 1951 to March 1952. There were candidates from seventy-seven political parties and a large number of independents. Polling was well-organized and, according to all observers, fair. The people of India responded to Jawaharlal's faith in them in a manner that was dramatic and magnificent. They saw the franchise as a special privilege, and turned out in large numbers to vote. Voting day became a kind of carnival, setting a trend for the future. Predictably, the Congress won overwhelmingly. It was Jawaharlal's moment of triumph. Opponents within and without the Congress had attacked Jawaharlal before and during the campaign, so he could be excused if he thought that the people of India had reposed their trust not only in the Congress but in a Congress of which Jawaharlal was the leader. A sad beginning to his prime ministership notwithstanding, the first five years had clearly placed Jawaharlal at the helm of affairs.

Planning the Economy

Even before he became prime minister, Jawaharlal had been aware that many of India's political and social problems would fall into place if the all–important problem of India's economic progress was addressed and solved. In the very years of India's independence, he was acutely conscious of a crisis that threatened to overwhelm the very existence of India. He wrote to Patel: 'All I can do is to hope and work and pray' (Gopal: 2: 96). But even this looming danger could not divert his attention from the economy and its paramount importance. He was convinced that the government was doing too little to address the rising cost of living. To drive home the point, he wrote to the food minister with only a hint of hyperbole: 'Indeed I have almost come to the conclusion that it would be a good thing if we stopped all other work and concentrated on our economic and food policy'.

Jawaharlal was convinced that India could achieve meaningful economic progress if the state had a greater say in economic matters, and that this could only happen through systematic planning. 'Planning', he said in a speech, 'was science in action'. To this end, he created the Planning Commission in 1950. The purpose and the aims of planning acquired a new urgency and direction in the aftermath of the first elections and the formation of the new ministry. Production had to be increased but this alone was not enough; consumption and purchasing power needed to grow. These were interrelated processes. Significant development in production was required to generate employment opportunities for the majority of the people. Employment and income would push up demand, which, in turn, would spur production. Whatever restrictions existed in setting this process to work were to be removed. It was an investment for the future. So, on one hand, Jawaharlal was looking to build large industrial and infrastructural projects, which were at the very core of the planning process. On the other, he sought to introduce small schemes, cottage industries, and community development, which he believed, would enhance purchasing power and demand.

Jawaharlal added an ideological dimension to these programmes of economic development—the building of 'a socialistic pattern of society'. The term was vague, but in Jawaharlal's mind, it was linked to a specific mission: 'I will not rest content unless every man, woman and child in this country has a fair deal and attains a minimum standard of living'. He believed that this mission could be accomplished in a decade. The Second Five-Year Plan was geared to meet these aims. Rapid industrial development would lead to full employment, and thus to fundamental changes to the economic structure; society would reorient itself and look towards equality instead of hierarchy. The state would be the engine for driving forward heavy industries producing capital goods; the state would also finance the expansion of village industries for the production of consumer goods. Both sectors would provide employment. The assumption was that if enough goods were produced, deficit financing—the inevitable fallout of increasing state expenditure—would not inevitably lead to inflation.

A key element in Jawaharlal's way of thinking was the idea that at this stage of India's economic development, it was important for the state to control strategic areas of the production process. The eminent Indian economist, Sukhamoy Chakravarty, a key figure in the planning process in the 1970s and 1980s, wrote approvingly that 'he [Jawaharlal] viewed planning as a positive instrument for resolving conflict in a large and heterogeneous subcontinent' (Chakravarty 1987: 3). One consequence of this was the bureaucratization of the Planning Commission into a separate vested interest, with its own leverages of power and influence, and its increasing distance from the people and the democratic process.

The signs of this were already present in the Planning Commission's early years. It was originally set up as an advisory body with Jawaharlal as its chairman. But after 1955, the Planning Commission became an extension of the prime minister's authority in matters relating to economic policy. Its position and power increased, and there was an erasure of the distinction between the advisory role of the Commission and the decision-making responsibilities of the government. Members of the Commission were given ranks and privileges enjoyed by cabinet ministers. There was also an overlapping of officials: the cabinet secretary was the secretary of the Commission, while the chief economic advisor of the finance ministry, acted also as the economic advisor to the Planning Commission. The real power of the Planning Commission, though, lay in its close relationship with the prime minister. Jawaharlal, for example, frequently asked for cabinet approval of decisions he had already endorsed as chairman of the Planning Commission. Jawaharlal's economic policy was officially endorsed by the Congress and the Parliament. The Lok Sabha agreed in December 1954 that 'the objective of our economic policy should be a socialistic pattern of society; and toward this end the tempo of economic activity in general and industrial development in particular should be stepped up to the maximum extent possible'. In January 1955 at the Awadhi session of the Congress, Jawaharlal moved the resolution which wedded the party to the principle of planning and to the establishment of a socialistic pattern of society.

Thus, in terms of economic policy under Jawaharlal, the government committed itself to three objectives: self-sustained growth, reduction of inequality, and a socialistic pattern of society. This last goal stands in need of some clarification. One perspicacious commentator has noted:

> Whatever might have been its [the term socialist pattern] original conception, it is not easy to find an operational definition of the term ... It did not imply the setting up of a welfare state with substantial diversion of resources towards such sectors as health or education or subsidized consumption for the poor. Neither did it imply any significant interference with the existing structure of property or other institutional arrangements. There was hardly any nationalization and no confiscation of any kinds of assets. What it meant in effect was that the Government was to take an active part in certain kinds of economic activity; it meant the setting up of public sector industries. (Chaudhuri 1978: 217)

This decision to make the state a key player in the economy and the emphasis on industrialization was not made open to a public debate. These were political decisions taken at Jawaharlal's behest. The expertise for the economic model that was followed in the Second Five-Year Plan (1955–60) came largely from renowned statistician P.C. Mahalanobis. The technical sophistication of the model notwithstanding, it was subject to the demands of the political leadership. Amartya Sen noted this point in 1958 when he wrote, 'It really depends upon what you are after. If you are asked (by say, Pandit Nehru or Krushchev) whether a particular target, which the government wants to achieve, can be achieved, you can answer the question with a model of the Professor Mahalanobis sort' (cited in Khilnani 1997: 86). Perhaps Chakravarty wanted to suggest this as well, when he described Jawaharlal as the 'chief architect of Indian planning' (Chakravarty 1978: 3).

The strategy adopted in the Second Plan and the crucial role accorded to the state in it was consistent with the prevailing ideology of the Nehruvian era. At the heart of the plan was the idea of economic growth. India was a poor country, and the poverty could not be reduced substantially through redistribution. As Jawaharlal once said in a characteristic rhetorical flourish, 'in a poor country there is only poverty to redistribute' (cited in Chaudhuri 1987: 219). The requirement was a substantial increase in goods and services that were available in the economy. It was argued that output levels in India were low because of the deficiency of material capital that prevented the introduction of more productive technologies. The need was to increase capital formation through a high rate of investment. This required an increase in the stock of capital goods in the economy: that is how capital formation is related to the production of capital goods. The objective was to increase capital goods over a period of time, and hence, the strategy of diverting investments towards heavy industries came into being. Heavy industries, by definition, required large-scale investment. Under the conditions prevailing in India in the 1950s, such a requirement meant that private enterprise would hesitate in making this kind of investment. Moreover, the market for these kinds of goods was non-existent. This would also keep out private capital. Therefore, it was argued, this kind of investment would have to come from the government through public sector enterprises (Chaudhuri 1987: 216–18). This was completely in tune with the vision of a socialistic pattern of society that Jawaharlal upheld.

Whatever be the merits and demerits of what has come to be known as the Nehru–Mahalanobis strategy, it was clear by the mid-1960s, during the immediate aftermath of Jawaharlal's death, that India faced an economic crisis. The Third Plan period (1961–6) had not registered any increase in per capita income, as population growth had cancelled out low overall gains in the rate of growth of national income. Availability of food grains and other essential items per capita was at or below 1956 levels. Agricultural output was unchanged between 1961 and 1963, had moved upward in 1964, but had plummeted in the drought of 1965. Inflation was spiralling as prices of food articles had increased by 32 per cent despite record imports of 25 million tons of food grains over the five years of the Plan. Industrial production had slowed down because of low levels of demand and shortages of domestic raw materials. The creation of additional capacity in industries like steel, engineering goods, and chemicals had not helped. In the first years of the Plan, average growth rates had varied between 8 and 10 per cent but had declined to a little over 4 per cent in 1965–6. Unemployment was estimated at 12 million at the end of the Plan period. The shortage of food reached alarming proportions in 1966, and statutory rationing had to be introduced in Kerala and in all large cities and towns, covering 30 million persons. Another 200 million were covered by the extension of fair price shops. But these schemes could not stop price rise. The balance of payments situation was precarious and the suspension of US aid hindered the government's attempts to import raw materials, machinery, and spare parts (Frankel 1978: 293–4). The vision of planned state-driven self-sustained growth had become a chimera. The author of the strategy, Mahalanobis, acknowledged that the strategy had failed. Reflecting on the experience in 1969, he wrote, 'India's promised social and economic revolution failed to materialize' (cited in Khilnani 1997: 86–7): no take-off, no industrial revolution, no self-generating growth.

Foreign Policy

Even before Jawaharlal as prime minister had had the time to formulate a foreign policy, save a vague hope that India should have a place in world affairs, he was forced into a contentious issue. This was to do with Kashmir. The Maharaja of Kashmir in August 1947 was Hari Singh, who, at the best of times, was not a very competent ruler, preferring horse racing to administration. But as India and Pakistan attained independence, he was forced into a situation where he had to make a choice: to join India or Pakistan. In terms of geographical location, it made more sense to join Pakistan. But Singh was loath to join a Muslim state. If he joined India, his subjects, many of them Muslims, would resent the decision. Also, Singh feared that by joining India, given Congress's commitment to democracy and its attitude towards the princely states, he would be eroding his own power and position. So he played for time by signing a 'standstill agreement' with India and offering a similar one to Pakistan. He thus stalled the question of accession and hoped that he would be able to retain Kashmir's independence.

The Government of India did not respond to the 'standstill agreement' for the simple reason that it was received too late in Delhi, when trouble in Kashmir had already started. Jawaharlal's reaction to the stalemate in Kashmir was to advise the Kashmiri authorities to invite Sheikh Abdullah of the National Conference, a hugely popular political party in the Kashmir valley, to form a provisional government and announce fresh elections. Accession was not uppermost in Jawaharlal's mind. Within Kashmir, the Muslim Conference represented the view that Kashmir should join Pakistan and campaigned vigorously for it. They were helped by Muslim League activists from Pakistan. Matters took a precipitous turn when, on 22 October 1947, nearly 5,000 tribesmen entered Kashmir from Pakistan and moved towards Srinagar. Hari Singh's options were now closed. He offered to accede to India and formally asked the government of India for military assistance.

Jawaharlal was convinced that the invasion had taken place with the full assistance of Pakistani authorities. In the meeting of the Indian Defence Committee on October 25, the military chiefs were directed to send weapons and ammunition to Kashmir and to prepare for action. The next day, after hearing that the situation was serious from V.P. Menon, a bureaucrat who had worked closely with Patel in bringing the princely states into the Indian Union and who had been despatched to Srinagar, the Defence Committee decided to airlift troops to Srinagar. India accepted Hari Singh's offer to join India with the condition that people's wishes would be ascertained once hostilities ceased in Kashmir. Singh appointed Abdullah the head of the emergency administration. It appears, therefore, that at this stage, Jawaharlal was more concerned with the establishment of a democratic process in Kashmir than with the state's accession to India.

The situation, however, ran swiftly out of control. The fighting escalated as Jinnah, against the advice of British officials, refused to accept the legality of the accession. Negotiations began with Mountbatten flying to Lahore to meet Jinnah. He carried a resolution passed by the Defence Committee that stated that the question of accession should 'be decided by an impartial reference to the will of the people'. Jawaharlal added that to ensure impartiality that elections [to find out the will of the people] 'should be held under United Nations auspices' after '*complete law and order have been established*' (Raghavan 2017: 110; emphasis added). Jinnah remained obstinately opposed to India's proposals, including the idea of plebiscite and particularly to Abdullah being in power. Pakistan's position on Abdullah was that he was a 'quisling' and an 'agent of the Congress for many years' (Raghavan 2017: 113).

Jawaharlal remained committed to armed action, and at one point even advocated the bombing of tribal concentrations on the Indian side of the border. At the same time, he was also increasingly becoming wary of the cost of war and was also acutely conscious that the situation in Kashmir could not be delinked from the negotiations in Hyderabad. He adopted a two-pronged approach: one, a reference to the United Nations; and two, complete military preparations to meet any eventuality. There was pressure from Mountbatten to stop all military action: in a letter, Mountbatten urged Jawaharlal '*to stop the fighting and to stop it as soon as possible*' (Raghavan 2017: 123). Jawaharlal never ruled out an escalation of military intervention, but he was cautious. One important factor in Jawaharlal's considerations was the cost of war. But there was another factor weighing on Jawaharlal's mind, seldom noted: his commitment to the democratic processes in Kashmir. In a letter to Hari Singh in December 1947, Jawaharlal wrote:

[I]t is of the most vital importance that Kashmir should remain within the Indian Union ... But however much we may want this, it cannot be done ultimately except through the goodwill of the mass of the population. Even if military forces held Kashmir for a while, a later consequence might be a strong reaction against this. Essentially, therefore this is a problem of psychological approach to the mass of the people and of making them feel they will be benefited by being in the Indian Union. If the average Muslim feels that he has no safe or secure place in the Union, then obviously he will look elsewhere. Our basic policy must keep this in view, or else we fail. (Guha 2007: 71–2)

Of course, it is easy to read this letter as a statement of Jawaharlal's weakness or his willingness to compromise on Kashmir. What is more important, perhaps, is the emphasis that he put on the will of the people and the idea of Kashmir.

There were two other reasons for Jawaharlal's unwillingness to push through a military solution. One was that by the beginning of 1948, it seemed that things were turning in India's favour in Kashmir. The other was that the government of India, on the advice of the then governor-general, Lord Mountbatten, had decided to take the Kashmir issue to the United Nations. The expectation was that since Kashmir had acceded to India, the United Nations could help clear what was considered an illegal occupation by groups sponsored by Pakistan. In the United Nations, things went against India, and very soon Jawaharlal rued the fact of taking the matter to the United Nations where in the Security Council, the matter was no longer being discussed as the 'Jammu and Kashmir Question' but as the 'India–Pakistan Question'. Jawaharlal was shocked by the bias exhibited by the USA and Britain in favour of Pakistan. Military operations recommenced in the summer of 1948 with India making significant gains in critical areas. But a completely military solution was not considered a feasible option in the cold Himalayan region, especially as winter approached. The situation was left to fester with a contentious Line of Control, across which was an arc of Pakistan-held territory, called Azad Kashmir by Pakistan and Pakistan Occupied Kashmir by India. The battle for Kashmir had no winners, only victims.

While an armed conflict in the opening years of his prime ministership had bruised Jawaharlal, the closing years of his tenure badly wounded him with another conflict. The military encounter with China in 1962, humiliating for India in all ways, was waiting to happen, since neither country accepted the borders that the British had drawn up. India believed that the treaty made in 1914 was valid, but the Chinese did not. The two governments thus proceeded from different and contradictory assumptions. The situation was aggravated and complicated by two developments: first, the Chinese invasion and takeover of Tibet in 1950;

and second, the Dalai Lama's escape from Tibet to seek asylum in India in 1959. Moreover, Jawaharlal, contrary to the views of some of his advisors, believed that China harboured no hostile intentions towards India. The Chinese, in turn, did not take kindly to India opening its doors to the Dalai Lama. Although India did not reckon that the takeover of Tibet was enough of a cause to show belligerence towards China, these factors formed the undercurrent to the apparently cordial and prolonged discussions that Jawaharlal had with his Chinese counterpart, Zhou Enlai. These discussions led nowhere, perhaps because the two leaders were working on different sets of assumptions, but Jawaharlal remained convinced about China's overall goodwill towards India.

Diplomacy and discussions were, however, completely overtaken by what was happening at the Sino-Indian border. It is clear from available documentation that both the countries, despite protestations of friendship across the negotiation table, were pursuing a 'forward policy' in sections of the long border—each trying to push the frontier to its advantage and to lay claims on more territory. On the Indian side, this forward policy had the sanction of both the civilian and military authorities, though they warned in no uncertain terms that if the situation escalated from skirmishes to a war, India was not prepared to defend its positions because of lack of resources, equipment, and logistic support. Srinath Raghavan comments that the army chiefs were unable to formulate specific proposals to meet Chinese incursions in Ladakh and this left the initiative of planning in the hands of the civilians (Raghavan 2017: 273).

At that point—in November 1961—Jawaharlal's view was that there would be no major military confrontation with the Chinese. There is no doubt that Jawaharlal was aware of the developments, since he had been briefed by the head of the Intelligence Bureau, B.N. Mullick. Jawaharlal was cautious as he did not want to run the risk of escalation. But he did not hesitate to stop Chinese incursions—the plan was to prevent these invasions by installing posts and increased patrolling aimed at convincing the Chinese that there would be resistance from the Indian side. The army chiefs still held the view that the Indian armed forces were not equipped to defend Indian positions across the Sino-Indian border. But they did not convey their reservations strongly enough to the prime minister. A critical reason for the army chiefs' reticence was that they had no alternatives to offer.

As a consequence of this 'forward policy', India established between May and July 1962 thirty-four additional paramilitary posts close to the border. In the northeast—North East Frontier Agency, as it was then called—India chose to be particularly aggressive. At a meeting chaired by the defence minister on 10 and 11 September 1962, it was decided that the Chinese forces from parts of the North East Frontier Agency must be expelled. The military was not convinced about the move, but the views of the political leaders prevailed. Jawaharlal's position was strangely ambiguous. He declared to his officials: '[W]e must take—or appear to take—a strong stand irrespective of consequences.' He said India had little option save evicting the Chinese '*or at least try to do so to the best of our abilities*' (Raghavan 2017: 297; emphasis by Jawaharlal). This would suggest that the prime minister was aware that India could only make a show of force instead of substantive action. It was a disaster waiting to happen.

The Chinese retaliated in both Ladakh and North East Frontier Agency, and wiped out the Indian forward posts. While there was a semblance of resistance in Ladakh to the advancing Chinese army, the Indian army collapsed in North East Frontier Agency without a fight. In November, the Chinese army was poised to enter the plains of Assam, and Leh in Ladakh. But much to everyone's surprise—including that of the clueless Government of India—the Chinese declared a unilateral ceasefire on 21 November and withdrew its troops to 1960 positions.

The 1962 Sino-Indian clash—'the war that wasn't', as one author (Verma 2016) has described it—was lowest point of Jawaharlal's prime ministership. As the holder of the top job, he could not avoid bearing the responsibility for the debacle. He did not even try to. There were a number of factors that determined the plight Jawaharlal found himself in. He had been convinced that the Chinese harboured no hostilities towards; he had believed this contrary to what some of his military advisors—most importantly, General K.S. Thimmayya—maintained. He also continued to believe, when a military confrontation seemed imminent, that a Sino-Indian clash would not remain a regional and a restricted affair but would acquire global dimensions, and that the Chinese would never risk such an outcome. Jawaharlal was utterly wrong on this point: he had not reckoned the fact that in the autumn of 1962, with the Cuban Missile Crisis looming over it, the Soviet Union could have ill afforded to alienate China. Indian decision makers, including the prime minister, had completely misread the Cold War context of the dispute and the eventual military encounter with China. There was also the inexplicable confidence of some of Jawaharlal's trusted officials, especially his defence minister and loyal lieutenant, Krishna Menon, towards whom Jawaharlal had a blind spot. It would also appear that the army chiefs—among whom, in 1961–2, were some of Jawaharlal and Menon's hand-picked generals—did not hammer home the point regarding

India's unpreparedness and China's military superiority. They went along with an untenable 'forward policy'. The outcome of all this was humiliation for India and the prime minister.

5

Envoi

Jawaharlal never quite recovered from the shock and setback of the Sino-Indian military clash and its humiliating outcome. In the beginning of 1964, he suffered a stroke, and died in May. The man who had been in the glow of health a few years ago had become the ghost of his energetic self in the months before his death. Such was his stature as prime minister that many educated persons in India wondered what would happen to India in his permanent absence. In his time, he had been a radical and youthful leader of the Congress, Gandhi's chosen heir and disciple and eventually the prime minister of the new Republic of India. It is justified to see Jawaharlal and his achievements through the prism of his political activities. But he was more than a towering political leader. One field of accomplishments without which

Jawaharlal can never be fully appreciated or understood is his career as a writer.

Jawaharlal, a keen reader ever since he was a schoolboy, became a writer while he served long prison sentences. Two of his major books—*An Autobiography* and *The Discovery of India*—were prison books. In the course of his political activities, Jawaharlal came to recognize that he was completely cut off from the life and education of his only daughter, Indira. He found a unique way to compensate for this anguish and alienation. He began to write regular letters to her in 1928 when Indira was in Mussoorie and Jawaharlal lived in the plains. These were no ordinary letters that a father writes to a daughter. The letters had the express aim of enriching his daughter's education—to inform her about the making of the world and its history, and also to provide for her a perspective to look at the history of the world. He wrote simply so that his daughter, a child of ten, easily understood what he was saying about the origins of the earth, the beginnings of life, and human prehistory. But circumstances prevented him from going beyond the coming of the Aryans, the formation of religious ideas, and the emergence of class. He published these letters in 1929 as *Letters from a Father to a Daughter*—his first book. It was a small book but well received. It is equally important to note that it stood the test of time.

The reception of his first book gave Jawaharlal the encouragement to continue writing letters while he was in prison in the early 1930s. These letters came to form a much larger volume—*Glimpses of World History*. The letters were about the development of human history from the Indus Valley Civilization to Jawaharlal's own times. He wrote them over three years. In a reflective preface to the first edition, Jawaharlal wrote:

> The letters are personal and there are many intimate touches in them which were meant for my daughter alone ... Physical inactivity leads to introspection and varying moods. I am afraid these changing moods are very apparent in the course of these letters, and the method of treatment is not the objective one of a historian. I do not claim to be a historian.

He saw the letters as 'superficial sketches' which were joined together by 'a thin thread'. What was this thread? It was the belief that history told the story of humanity's progress. In a letter dated 1 January 1933, he wrote: 'Man, in spite of his great and vaunted progress is still a very unpleasant and selfish animal. And yet perhaps it is possible to see the silver lining of progress right through the long and dismal record of selfishness and quarrelsomeness and inhumanity of man' (GWH: 552). Some of the letters he wrote show his gradual conversion to the materialist conception of history. He explicated to his daughter the basic tenets of Marxism and communism, and wrote admiringly about the success of Soviet planning. This faith in human progress, growing from the liberal and Fabian ideas, and values that he had imbibed from his wide-ranging reading, remained with Jawaharlal as a pillar of intellectual sustenance.

The mood of introspection that living in a prison cell engendered in Jawaharlal was most marked in the next book he wrote—his autobiography, completed around 1935 and published in 1936. It was written to break the ennui of prison life. He began writing it, as he remarked in the preface, 'in a mood of self-questioning'. In this book, Jawaharlal wanted to reflect upon what was happening in India and about his own involvement in those events and developments. This was mirrored in the full title of the book: *An Autobiography with Musings on Recent Events in India.* The book, by virtue of being an autobiography, was personal. But because the author was also an important political actor, politics inevitably formed a major part of the narrative about the author's life. However, politics never drowned the personal voice; rather, when the occasion demanded, it merged seamlessly with the personal. The book, unlike more famous autobiographies—one is reminded of those by Augustine, Rousseau, and Gandhi—was not confessional. It had nothing to tickle the curiosity of the prurient. The tone of the book—in keeping with Jawaharlal's penchant for introspection—was detached and laid-back. The style was austere. He did not assume any self-importance: the impression that the book conveys is that the author's life acquires importance because of the context and the circumstances. The personal gets salience because of the historical. Again, Jawaharlal was careful to warn his readers that his book was not a work of history. It merely traced the trajectory of his mental development. His assessments of situations were open-ended and nuanced. The colour of the book was grey rather than stark black and white. There was doubt, self-criticism, and self-scrutiny, with no straining towards certainty.

Looking back on his life, he admitted:

> If I were given the chance of going through my life again, with my present knowledge and experience added, I would no doubt try to make many changes in my personal life; I would endeavour to improve in many ways on what I have previously done, but my major decisions in public affairs would remain untouched. Indeed I could not vary them, for they were stronger than myself, and a force beyond my control drove me to them.

He was conscious of the impersonal forces of history and it was this awareness that perhaps prevented him from sketching any grand vision for the future. He commented with great perspicacity that 'the future has to be lived before it can be written about'. The future had no prepared text.

The personal inadequacies that Jawaharlal referred to grew, in part, from his upbringing. He commented thus on his plight:

I have become a queer mixture of the East and West, out of place everywhere, at home nowhere. Perhaps my thoughts and approach to life are more akin to what is called Western rather than Eastern but India clings to me, as she does to all her children, in innumerable ways ... I cannot get rid of either that past inheritance or my recent acquisitions. They are both part of me, and though they help me in both the East and the West, they also create in me a feeling of spiritual loneliness not in public activities but in life itself. I am a stranger and alien in the West. I cannot be of it. But in my own country also, sometimes, I have an exile's feeling.

An Autobiography was the best book Jawaharlal wrote, but any discussion of his autobiography would be incomplete without a few words on its dedication and its implication. The book was dedicated to his wife with the simple words: 'To Kamala who is no more'. The words were an assertion of a love that Jawaharlal had recognized far too late. As discussed previously, their marriage had never been an easy one. Kamala did not come from a wealthy and westernized family. When Motilal selected her to be his only son's bride, Kamala spoke no English, only Hindi and Urdu. Motilal brought her to Allahabad, before the wedding, and arranged to tutor her in English and Western modes of behaviour and table manners so that she could be a proper wife for his Cambridge-returned son. This social distance never quite left the married life of Kamala and Jawaharlal. Kamala accepted that Jawaharlal's political activities and frequent imprisonments would keep him away from her, but sometimes she found it difficult to cope with her loneliness. She admired her husband and his commitment, but there is no evidence to show that Jawaharlal attempted to understand her pain and to reach out to her. His introverted nature, reinforced by his training in Harrow and Cambridge, stood in the way showing his emotions. Thus, the initial distance was never bridged.

In the early 1930s, Kamala was critically ill, leading to the break down of Jawaharlal's stoicism. His prison diaries of this period are full of references to her and to her illness. He also began to realize the distance between himself and her. One entry (19 March 1935) reads:

What a child K is! That irritates me often enough and yet I think that is partly her charm. How my moods change when I think of her. How much she means to me and yet how little she fits in or tries to fit in with my ideas. That is really the irritating part, that she does not try, and so she drifts apart. (JNSW: 6: 331)

Jawaharlal's belated discovery of Kamala was best expressed in the last lines of poetry he gave her:

Thou wast all that to me, love,
For which my soul did pine—
A green isle in the sea, love,
A fountain and a shrine,
All wreathed with fairy fruits and flowers,
And all the flowers were mine.
And all my days are trances
And all my nightly dreams
Are where the grey eye glances,
And where thy footsteps gleams—
In what ethereal dances
By what eternal streams. (JNSW: 6: 296)

Jawaharlal was devastated by the death of Kamala on 28 February 1936. Throughout his life after her death, whether in a jail cell or in his bedroom, he kept a picture of Kamala and a small portion of her ashes. He left the request that Kamala's ashes be mingled with his after his death.

Jawaharlal's Western sensibilities were an obstacle to an appreciation of religion—a vital facet of Indian culture. He saw himself as a modern and rational individual for whom religion had little appeal since 'almost always it [religion] seems to stand for blind belief and reaction, dogma and bigotry, superstition and exploitation, and the preservation of vested interests'. Yet he was aware that religion had been the balm to 'innumerable tortured souls'. What concerned him most was that his disaffinity with religious sensibilities alienated him from large sections of the Indian people. He wrote with a dash of poignancy, 'I felt lonely and homeless, and India, to whom I had given my love and for whom I had laboured, seemed a strange and bewildering land to me. Was it my fault that I could not enter into the spirit and ways of thinking of my countrymen?' The most remarkable feature of the autobiography was noted by none other than Rabindranath Tagore, who, after reading the book, wrote to Jawaharlal: 'Through all its details there runs a deep current of humanity which overpasses the tangle of facts and leads us to the person who is greater than his deeds and truer than his surroundings' (Nehru 1958: 187).

The Discovery of India was Jawaharlal's third and arguably his most important book. It was written in the early 1940s when he was serving his longest prison sentence. By this time, Jawaharlal had sloughed off the detachment of *An Autobiography*. He wrote a more passionate and emotional book—*The Discovery of India*—in which he tried to evoke the greatness and uniqueness of India's past. Jawaharlal wrote to emphasize the continuity and the vitality of India's culture. There was a strong propensity in the book to idealize things that were Indian. The text suggests that the author, who, in his autobiography, had described his thoughts and approach to life to be Western, wanted to turn away and reinvent himself by discovering his Indian roots. He was still committed to the India of transforming India and making it into a modern nation, but also felt a pull towards his own and true heritage. He wrote to invoke pride in India's past. Isolated in jail at a time when nationalism in India was in its doldrums and a battle was raging across the world to preserve civilization from Nazi barbarism, Jawaharlal probably felt he needed a heavy dose of nationalist pride to keep his spirits afloat. The book became an emotional cradle for Jawaharlal. Its message and purpose were more significant than the mode of its argument, in which emotion prevailed over reason. The purpose of the book was evident from the epigraph, taken from Shakespeare's sonnet number thirty: 'When to the sessions of sweet silent thought/ I summon up remembrance of things past'. In the 1930s 'silent thought'—the solitude of a jail cell had engendered reasoned self-reflection. In the early 1940s the prevailing and all-encompassing gloom, solitude produced a gush of emotion.

★★★

Jawaharlal's political legacy falls into two separate but interconnected periods. One was the period before India's independence, and the second, his term as prime minister. Through the 1930s and 1940s, he emerged as one of Gandhi's most trusted lieutenants in the Indian national movement. He had come to the national movement following Jallianwala Bagh as a somewhat sceptical follower of Gandhi. His 'wandering among the kisans' of eastern United Provinces during the Non-Cooperation Movement had an enormous impact on him. It convinced him of the importance of non-violence and the Gandhian methods of protest, strengthened his commitment to the movement, and radicalized him. His exposure to European politics and ideas enabled him to link India's freedom struggle and his own radicalism to global movements against imperialism. Jawaharlal, even at this early stage, was convinced that India could not achieve its destiny by remaining isolated from the world. This conviction made him push within the Congress to put complete independence on the top of the party's agenda. This was his major contribution when he was the president of the Congress in 1929. In the next decade, he attempted to add another dimension to the goal of attaining complete independence. This was the idea of socialism to which Jawaharlal had been converted as he witnessed the rise of fascism in Europe and the success of planning in the Soviet Union. Jawaharlal tried to inject socialism and economic equality into the agenda of the Congress. This did not win him too many friends among the old leaders of the Congress including Vallabhbhai Patel, Rajendra Prasad, and even Gandhi, but it touched the hearts of many younger members of the Congress who looked up to Jawaharlal as their spokesman. Jawaharlal continued to believe that political freedom would be meaningless and without substance unless it came with economic freedom. He was convinced that only through socialism could the latter be achieved. As a continuation of these convictions, Jawaharlal became an advocate of industrialization and modern science and technology. He was conscious, as was Gandhi, that these ideas were contrary to most of Gandhi's fundamental tenets as explicated in *Hind Swaraj*.

Jawaharlal carried forward all these ideas into his prime ministership. He was convinced that these were essential components in the making of a new and independent nation. But over and above all this was his commitment to build democratic polity and society in India. He saw this commitment as his most important and initial responsibility. It was to that end that, contrary to all expectations and the surprise of many, he was an unswerving advocate of universal adult franchise. The first general elections of the Republic of India were held under these conditions—all adults had an equal voice in the building of India's future. Jawaharlal's commitment to democracy was evident in the importance he gave to the Parliament and its procedures. He led by example by being present in the Parliament as prime minister whenever the Parliament was in session and he was present in the capital. He took steps to establish the rule of law and the cabinet form of government in which the prime minister was *primus inter pares*. He anchored democracy in India on religious toleration and secularism, and ensured that India belonged to all Indians irrespective of their religious beliefs.

As an advocate of socialism and as the prime minister of a country in which the incidence of illiteracy was high and the penetration of education shallow, Jawaharlal believed that the state should be an active player in the society and the economy. Despite widespread hostility and controversy, he initiated reforms to change some aspects of the orthodox Hindu society. He was conscious that the orthodox Muslim society was also in need of reform, but did not venture into a reform programme because—in his view—there did not exist sufficient enlightenment and impetus for reform within the Muslim society. While the state attempted to reform the society, it was in the economic sphere that Jawaharlal made the state a key actor by (*a*) introducing planning where the state became the principal allocator of economic resources; (*b*) making the state owner of important manufacturing units to control the commanding heights of the economy; and (*c*) placing the state in charge of all major projects relating to the building of infrastructure. Jawaharlal believed that controlling the economy was the avenue to usher in socialism. He was conscious that India's path to economic self-sufficiency, and that modernity would not be viable without Indian technocrats and managers. To this end, the state under Jawaharlal invested in building institutes of technology and management that were modelled on international norms and standards.

From the time Jawaharlal was a young leader of the Congress, he had aspired to secure a place for India in the world. It was with this overall aspiration in mind that he approached the problem of fashioning India's foreign policy. It was here, perhaps, that he was the least successful. He had the misfortune of witnessing his foreign policy getting caught in the aggravating ambience of the Cold War. It was Jawaharlal's contention that as a fledgling nation, India should steer away from both poles of this covert war. He tried also to convince other Asian nations to do the same. This action propelled him to the position of a spokesman of a new Asia that believed it could build its own future since it had thrown off the shackles of Western domination.

The policy of non-alignment became one of the watchwords of Jawaharlal's foreign policy. An outcome of non-alignment was the Bandung Conference, which Jawaharlal described as a 'great achievement [that] proclaimed the political emergence in world affairs of over half the world's population. [But] it presented no unfriendly challenge or hostility to anyone' (cited in Guha 2007: 164). But Jawaharlal was not always consistent in the implementation of non-alignment. The policy was put to the test in 1956. In July that year, Gamal Abdel Nasser nationalized the company that managed the Suez Canal. Not surprisingly Britain, France, and Israel invaded Egypt to gain control over the canal. Jawaharlal criticized the invasion in strong terms. However, when a few weeks later, Soviet tanks rolled into Hungary to brutally suppress an anti-Soviet uprising, Jawaharlal was unwilling to condemn or criticize it. Indeed, during the vote in the United Nations, India abstained. Hence, the unkind, if somewhat justified, comment that the policy of 'friendly with all' was morphed into 'friendlier with some' (cited in Gopal: 2: 310). Jawaharlal professed to be a pacifist in world affairs, but did not hesitate to use the armed forces to annex Goa into the Indian Union. He left Kashmir and issues with Pakistan festering, and could not escape responsibility for the humiliation at the hands of the Chinese.

In many ways, Jawaharlal was an idealist, but he was not free from contradictions. His admiring biographer noted some of them while describing Jawaharlal as 'a Marxist who rejected regimentation, a socialist who was wholly committed to civil liberties, a radical who accepted non-violence, an international statesman with a total involvement in India, and above all, a leader who believed in carrying his people with him even if it slowed down the pace of progress' (FIJN: 792). He could have added that even though Jawaharlal was not a religious man as he so often emphasized in his writings, he sought 'some kind of ethical approach to life' (DoI: 17). But he was not quite sure what this ethical approach was. He wrote to Gandhi in May 1933:

> Religion is not familiar ground for me, and as I have grown older, I have definitely drifted away from it. I have something else in its place, something older than just intellect and reason, which gives me strength and hope. Apart from this indefinable and indefinite

121

urge, which may have just a tinge of religion in it and yet is wholly different from it, I have grown entirely to rely on the workings of the mind. Perhaps they are weak supports to rely upon but search as I will, I can see no better ones.

Jawaharlal was a political leader, by force of circumstances a mass political leader, who relied on the workings of the mind. His making of India could not but be an intellectual project; he thus left behind a legacy of intellectual, historical, and political understanding, which was grounded in empathy and religious tolerance, and a deep humanity.

Because of his intellectual orientation, he remained a democrat who was conscious of the immense popularity and power he commanded. His powers of self-reflection allowed him to make an extremely perceptive assessment of himself back in 1937. Under the *nom de plume* Chanakya, he wrote:'Jawaharlal cannot become a fascist. And yet he has all the makings of a dictator in him—vast popularity, a strong will directed to a well-defined purpose, energy, pride, organizational capacity, ability, hardness, and, with all his love of the crowd, an intolerance of others and a certain contempt for the weak and the inefficient' (JNEW: 2: 643–6). In 1942 at Ahmadnagar Fort, he noted a statement of Gautama Buddha in his diary:'I would enter a blazing fire but I would not entire my home with my goal unattained'. Jawaharlal added that as he read that line, 'a thrill passed through me, almost an electric shock' (FIJN: 788). In his twilight years, Jawaharlal was profoundly conscious of how much he had left undone. Thus, on his desk, he copied out and kept on his table those moving lines of Robert Frost: 'The woods are lovely, dark and deep,/ But I have promises to keep,/ And miles to go before I sleep,/And miles to go before I sleep' (Gopal: 3: 367). Once asked what his legacy to India would be, Jawaharlal had replied, 'Hopefully, it is four hundred million people capable of governing themselves' (Gopal: 3: 278).

India has miles to go to complete Jawaharlal's unfinished legacy.

References and Further Readings

Chakravarty, Sukhamoy. *Development Planning: The Indian Experience*. Oxford: Oxford University Press, 1987.

Chandra, Bipan. 'Jawaharlal Nehru and Indian Capitalist Class, 1936', in *Nationalism and Colonialism in Modern India*, edited by Bipan Chandra, pp. 187–200. New Delhi: Orient Blackswan, 1979.

Chaudhuri, P. *The Indian Economy: Poverty and Development*. London: Macmillan, 1978.

Frankel, F. *India's Political Economy: 1947–77*. Princeton: Princeton University Press, 1978.

Gandhi, Mohandas Karamchand. *Collected Works of Mahatma Gandhi*. New Delhi: Publications Division, 1958–1994.

Gandhi, Rajmohan. *Patel: A Life*. Ahmedabad: Navajivan Publishing House, 1991.

Gopal, Sarvepalli. *Jawaharlal Nehru: A Biography*, 3 vols. London and Delhi: Jonathan Cape and Oxford University Press, 1975–84.

_____. 'The Formative Ideology of Jawaharlal Nehru'. *Economic and Political Weekly* vol. 11, no. 21 (May 1976): 787–92.

Guha, Ramachandra. *India after Gandhi: The History of the World's Largest Democracy*. London: Picador, 2007.

Iyengar, Uma and Lalitha Zackariah (eds). *Together They Fought: Gandhi–Nehru Correspondence, 1921–1948*. New Delhi: Oxford University Press, 2011. (All letters between Gandhi and Nehru quoted in the text are taken from this collection. The dates of the letters are provided in the relevant citations.)

Khilnani, Sunil. *The Idea of India*. London: Michael Joseph, 1997.

Mukherjee, Rudrangshu. *Nehru & Bose: Parallel Lives*. New Delhi: Penguin, Viking, 2014.

Nehru, Jawaharlal. *An Autobiography*. London: Bodley Head, 1936.

_____. *Glimpses of World History*. Allahabad: Kitabistan, 1934–5; repr. New Delhi: Penguin Books, 2004.

_____. *The Discovery of India*. Calcutta: Signet Press, 1946.

_____. *A Bunch of Old Letters*. Bombay: Asia Publishing House, 1958.

_____. *Selected Works of Jawaharlal Nehru*, edited by Sarvepalli Gopal. New Delhi: Orient Longman and Oxford University Press, 1972–.

_____. *Essential Writings*, edited by Sarvepalli Gopal and Uma Iyengar. Delhi: Oxford University Press, 2003.

Nehru Papers. New Delhi: Nehru Memorial Museum and Library.

Raghavan, Srinath. *War and Peace in Modern India*. Ranikhet: Permanent Black and Ashoka University, 2017.

Roberts, Andrew. *'The Holy Fox': The Life of Lord Halifax*. London: Phoenix, 1991, repr. 2004.

Sarkar, Sumit. *Modern India: 1885–1947*. New Delhi: Macmillan, 1983.

Sitaramayya, B. Pattabhi. *The History of the Indian National Congress*, 2 vols. Bombay: Padma Publications, 1935, repr. 1946.

Som, Reba. *Differences within Consensus: The Left–Right Divide in the Congress, 1929–39*. New Delhi: Sangam, 1995.

Tendulkar, D.G. *Mahatma*, 8 vols. Bombay: Ministry of Information and Broadcasting, Government of India, 1951.

Verma, Shiv Kunal. *1962: The War That Wasn't: The Definitive Account of the Clash Between India and China*. New Delhi: Aleph, 2016.

Ziegler, Philip. *Mountbatten: The Official Biography*. London: Collins, 1985.

Short Guide to Further Reading

Jawaharlal Nehru's life and views are best accessed through his own writings, especially *An Autobiography* (London: The Bodley Head, 1936) and *The Discovery of India* (Calcutta: The Signet Press, 1946). Sarvepalli Gopal's *Jawaharlal Nehru: A Biography*, 3 vols (London and New Delhi: Jonathan Cape and Oxford

University Press, 1975–84) remains unsurpassed as a biography of Nehru, although the tone is generally uncritical, especially in Volumes 2 and 3, which cover the prime ministerial years. The context and the events of Nehru's premiership is very well covered in Ramachandra Guha's *India after Gandhi: The History of the World's Largest Democracy* (London: Picador, 2007), and also in Sunil Khilnani's *The Idea of India* (London: Michael Joseph, 1997). A very critical perspective on Nehru is provided by Partha Chatterjee in the chapter on him ('The Moment of Arrival: Nehru and the Passive Revolution') in *Nationalist Thought and the Colonial World: A Derivative Discourse?* (London: Zed Books, 1986). Sunil Khilnani is outstandingly perceptive on Nehru in two essays: 'Nehru's Faith'. *Economic and Political Weekly* vol. 37, no. 48 (30 November–6 December 2002); and 'Nehru's Judgement', in *Political Judgement: Essays for John Dunn*, edited by R. Bourke and R. Geuss (Cambridge: Cambridge University Press, 2009), pp. 254–78.

Some aspects of Nehru's foreign policy are covered in detail in Srinath Raghavan, *War and Peace in Modern India* (Ranikhet: Permanent Black, Ashoka University, repr. 2017). Nehru's relationship with Gandhi is best accessed through their correspondence available in Uma Iyengar, and Lalitha Zackariah (eds), *Together They Fought: Gandhi–Nehru Correspondence, 1921–1948*

(New Delhi: Oxford University Press, 2011). Nehru's relationship with Subhas Chandra Bose is discussed in Rudrangshu Mukherjee's *Nehru & Bose: Parallel Lives* (New Delhi: Penguin, Viking, 2014.)

Index

About the Author

Rudrangshu Mukherjee is chancellor and professor of history at Ashoka University, India, of which he had been the founding vice-chancellor. He has taught in the Department of History at the University of Calcutta. He has also held visiting appointments at Princeton University, Manchester University, and the University of California, Santa Cruz. Between 1993 and 2014, he had been editor, Editorial Pages, *The Telegraph*, Kolkata.

Mukherjee completed his schooling from Calcutta Boys' School, Kolkata, and went for further studies to Presidency College, Kolkata, Jawaharlal Nehru University, New Delhi, and St Edmund Hall, Oxford. He was awarded a DPhil in modern history by the University of Oxford. Some of his important publications are *Awadh in Revolt 1857–58: A Study of Popular Resistance* (1984, repr. 2002), *Spectre of Violence: The Kanpur Massacres in the Revolt of 1857* (1998, repr. 2007), *Year of Blood: Essays on 1857* (2014), *The Penguin*

Gandhi Reader (1993), *Great Speeches of Modern India* (2007), *Nehru & Bose: Parallel Lives* (2014), and *Twilight Falls on Liberalism* (2018).